The Complete Disciple

PAUL W. POWELL

While this book is designed for the reader's personal enjoyment, it is also intended for group study. A Leader's Guide with Victor Multiuse Transparency Masters is available from your local bookstore or from the publisher.

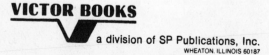
VICTOR BOOKS
a division of SP Publications, Inc.
WHEATON, ILLINOIS 60187

Offices also in Fullerton, California • Whitby, Ontario, Canada • Amersham-on-the-Hill, Bucks, England

Unless otherwise noted, Scripture quotations are from the *King James Version* (KJV).

Recommended Dewey Decimal Classification: 248.4
Suggested Subject Headings: CONDUCT OF CHRISTIAN LIFE

Library of Congress Catalog Card Number: 81-86105
ISBN: 0-88207-307-9

VICTOR BOOKS
A division of SP Publications, Inc.
P.O.Box 1825 ● Wheaton, Illinois 60187

Contents

DEDICATED TO

Mr. & Mrs. Steve Vaught

In-laws
who gave me my wife
who have enriched my life
and who have encouraged me in every way

FOREWORD

The proliferation of books on discipleship in our own era has had one noticeable deficiency. Most of the books have not come from the pens of the pastors of the churches. That is why I am exceptionally grateful that Dr. Paul W. Powell, pastor of the rapidly burgeoning Green Acres Baptist Church of Tyler, Texas, has written this book—*The Complete Disciple*. It is a fresh approach to Christian discipleship.

Dr. Powell has been serving various churches as pastor for more than 25 years. It is from this matrix that such a clear perception of biblical discipleship has come. No one can appreciate the long-term development of Christian discipleship like a man who has served for a quarter of a century as a pastor.

The second great asset of this book is an approach that is, in some sense of the word, novel. The approach is not novel in terms of the Scriptures, because they are unchangeable. Rather, the freshness of the approach is due to the unique understanding which Dr. Powell brings to the subject of the Christian's call. This is reflected in the very table of contents. Often it is said that a Christian is called by Christ, but what exactly is entailed? If you want to know what it means to be called of Christ to discipleship, you will discover it in these remarkable pages.

After you have completed the reading of *The Complete Disciple*, it is my persuasion that you will discover that you have grown spiritually as a result.

W. A. Criswell
Pastor's Study
First Baptist Church
Dallas, Texas

PREFACE

Jesus gave us two great symbols of commitment. Both of them were made of wood. One was the cross; the other was the yoke.

The cross and the yoke symbolize for us the two different aspects of commitment. The cross is an instrument of death; the yoke is an implement of toil. The cross is the symbol of sacrifice; the yoke is the symbol of service. The cross suggests blood; the yoke suggests sweat.

Christian commitment means that we are ready for either the cross or the yoke. When we follow Jesus it should be with such absolute surrender that we are ready to die for Him, or we are ready to work for Him. We are ready to bleed, or we are ready to sweat. We are ready to suffer, or we are ready to serve—whichever He may require.

If I were asked to draw a symbol for Christian commitment it would be a picture of a cross on one hand, a yoke on the other, and a Christian on his knees between them saying, "Ready for either."

This book deals with the cost of that commitment. Without a doubt, Christ gives many benefits to those who follow Him. He gives us forgiveness, peace, purpose, power, and hope.

But He also makes stringent demands on us. That's what this book is about—the demands of discipleship.

Christ is still calling us to commitment today. His call is the same as it was in the first century—to the cross and to the yoke. I hope as you understand what this means that you will answer His call to total commitment.

1

Called to a Yoke

Jesus used two great symbols for Christian commitment. The first is quite familiar to us; the second is virtually unknown. Can you guess what they are?

The first is a cross. The second is a yoke. Some people wear crosses as ornaments around their necks. And crosses are commonly found on the steeples of churches everywhere. The cross more than anything else is a symbol of Christianity.

The yoke, however, is almost unknown among Christians. I have never seen a yoke worn as an ornament around anyone's neck or placed on the steeple of any church. Yet it, as much as the cross, is a symbol of commitment to Jesus Christ.

Jesus spoke of the cross when He said, "Whosoever will come after Me, let him deny himself, and take up his cross, and follow Me" (Mark 8:34). He spoke of the yoke when He said, "Take My yoke upon you, and learn of Me" (Matt. 11:29).

The cross is an instrument of death; the yoke is an implement of toil. The cross is a symbol of sacrifice; the yoke is a symbol of service. The cross suggests blood; the yoke suggests sweat. Put them both together and you have an idea of

7

what Christian commitment is all about.

To be committed to Jesus Christ means that we are ready for either the yoke or the cross. We are ready to die on the cross or we are ready to pull on the yoke. We are ready to bleed for him or we are ready to sweat for Him. We are ready to sacrifice or we are ready to serve.

Jesus called us to a yoke when He said, "Come unto Me, all ye that labor and are heavy laden, and I will give you rest. Take My yoke upon you, and learn of Me; for I am meek and lowly in heart; and ye shall find rest unto your souls. For My yoke is easy, and My burden is light" (Matt. 11:28-30).

This is one of the clearest calls to personal commitment to be found in all the Scriptures. These words were addressed to people who were weary and defeated by life. And their religion was of no help to them. Instead of helping to lift their burdens, it added to them. Their ceremonial, legalistic religion was like weights, not wings.

Jesus gave this great invitation to us, as well as to those people. Many do not know God the Father, and so they are restless, searching, and unfulfilled. They are not committed to any great cause and so their lives lack purpose and meaning. You might be like that yourself. If you are longing for rest from the terror, power, and drudgery of sin, I have good news for you. Jesus invites you to come to Him. If you do, He will enable you to live abundantly, joyfully, and triumphantly.

However, a word of caution is in order. You must first trust in Him. Then you must take His yoke upon you. You must become His disciple.

A yoke is a harness made of wood by which two animals are tied together to pull a load. The yoke suggests submission, obedience, and service. To take the yoke of Christ upon us means that we submit to His leadership and to His lordship. It means that we surrender our lives to His will.

So Christ's call to commitment is a call to the yoke. It is a call to surrender, to submit, to yield to Him. Three things

are involved in taking His yoke upon us: decision, discipleship, and deliverance.

Called to Decision

The first step to commitment is to *recognize Jesus Christ as
the Son of God and begin following Him*. It is only in Him
and through Him that we can find God.

This great invitation of Jesus begins with the word *come*.
This is one of our Lord's favorite words. He used it when He
invited Peter and Andrew to be His disciples. He said,
"Come ye after Me, and I will make you to become fishers
of men" (Mark 1:17).

Jesus again used the word *come* when He invited ittle
children to be brought to Him. He said, "Suffer the little
children to come unto Me, and forbid them not; for of such
is the kingdom of God" (Mark 10:14).

He used it again in the closing invitation of the Bible.
There He said, "And the Spirit and the bride say, Come.
And let him that heareth say, Come. And let him that is
athirst come. And whosoever will, let him take of the water
of life freely" (Rev. 22:17).

The invitation is to come to Jesus personally. The "I" in
His call is emphatic. He Himself will give us rest. Jesus is the
end of our search for God; He is the end of our restlessness
and our longings. He alone is the object of our faith and our
devotion.

The essence of Christianity is that Jesus Christ is God. He
is not just a part of God. He is not just sent from God. He is
not just related to God. He was and is God.

Several years ago a young Jewish man began attending
worship services at our church. He showed a deep interest in
Christianity, so I took him to lunch one day and shared my
faith with him. As he continued to attend worship services I
could almost see him change week by week.

One Sunday morning in our worship services we sang the
Gospel song, "On Christ the Solid Rock I Stand." Martin
joined in and sang with great gusto. As he did, his whole

body literally swayed to the rhythm of the music. When the service was over he asked me if he could buy one of our hymnals. He told me that he bought tapes of our worship services and listened to them every morning. He wanted a hymnbook so he could sing along with the congregation as he listened to the tapes.

A few days later we had lunch together again. This time he shared his spiritual quest with me. He had been in Florida a year earlier and had become so despondent over his life that he had attempted suicide. Someone in the Salvation Army found him and saved his life. When he was well he returned home to Tyler, Texas. He knew there had to be more to life than he had found up till then, so he began to search for God. Martin's father was a regular listener to the radio broadcasts of our Sunday morning worship services. Martin had noticed a remarkable change in his father but did not know what had caused it.

Martin also began to listen to the broadcasts of our services. At the same time he plunged into the faith of his fathers with great zeal. A religious holiday approached and so in obedience to his faith, he fasted all day and then went to the synagogue for worship that night. He said, "When I left the synagogue that night, I felt nothing but physical hunger and spiritual emptiness. I walked outside, leaned up against a tree, and wept aloud, saying, 'Oh, God, I'm so empty. There must be more to life than this.'"

That's when he began attending our church. Then he leaned over the table and said to me with a broad smile on his face, "Paul, I have found the Messiah."

The next Sunday he professed faith in Christ. That night I baptized him. He told me that when I lifted him out of the water he wanted to shout to the world, "Hallelujah! God lives! God lives!"

Martin had discovered something we all need to know. It is Jesus, not religion, that we need. Jesus came in fact to make religion unnecessary. And only He can fill the emptiness in us. That's why He invites us to come to Him.

Coming to Christ is a personal and decisive act. It is a choice that every person has to make for himself. Have you ever come to Jesus Christ and found the peace and rest that you're looking for? Many people who have walked the aisles and met the pastor have never met the Master. If you have never come to Christ, then come today.

Called to Discipleship

Jesus not only invites us to come to Him, but He also tells us to *take His yoke upon us so that we may learn of Him* (Matt. 11:29).

These two acts—coming to Him and taking His yoke on us—describe two separate stages of commitment which every believer needs to take. By taking His yoke upon us, we become His disciples.

Through the centuries millions of people have come to Christ and have found the salvation He promised. But many of them failed to take up the yoke of submission and to find the complete rest He promises. They received Jesus as Saviour, but they did not submit to Him as Lord.

It is only as we yield to Christ and get under His yoke that we can learn of Him. When I was a boy I used to enjoy visiting my grandparents' farm. My grandfather had two plow horses that I especially liked. They were good work animals, but they could not know the mind of my grandfather without being in harness.

However, when they were in harness, he could direct them and make his will known to them. Through submission to the harness, they understood what my grandfather wanted them to do.

Submission to Christ's yoke or harness is never easy. It means death to self and that is always hard. Most of us want to serve God but in an advisory capacity only. Submission is contrary to our very nature. The essence of sin is rebellion. The Bible says, "All we like sheep have gone astray; we have turned every one to his own way" (Isa. 53:6). We are all basically rebellious and selfish.

Don't think that your husband is the only stubborn man in town. Don't think that your children are the only rebellious kids on the block. Don't think that your wife is the only headstrong woman around. Don't think that your boss is the most hard-nosed person in the world. We are all that way. And this is the root of all of our problems.

Leighton Ford tells about a friend who was giving a series of lectures at a university. After one of the talks, he discussed Christianity with a young mathematics teacher. As he talked about the Christian faith, he explained to the man that if he committed his life to Jesus he would have to move over and let Jesus take the center. The young teacher thought about that for a moment and then blurted out, "I'm very reluctant for this decentralization."

Decentralization is a good term for commitment, if you use its secondary definition, "to cause to withdraw from the center." Nothing less than this is meant after a person becomes a Christian and starts living as a Christian. To take Jesus' yoke upon us means that Jesus takes control of our lives.

True commitment is not measured by our orthodoxy, nor by our involvement in a Christian organization, but by our obedience to Christ. God does not give rest simply to those who believe in Him or desire Him but to those who obey Him.

Submission to Christ expresses itself in practical ways. A minister of music told me of his submission to the lordship of Christ. He said, "I died to self and stopped singing music that fed my ego and started singing music that ministered to people."

Sam Shoemaker quoted a man as saying, "Submission costs, and since I think quite a lot of myself it costs me quite a lot." To submit to Christ's yoke means to yield our wills to His will.

It is only as we come to Christ, submit to Christ, and learn of Christ that we receive from Christ the rest that He promises.

Called to Deliverance

Jesus promises rest to all those who follow Him. *He promises to deliver us, if we depend on Him, from the weariness and frustration of empty lives.* He assures us that His yoke is easy and His burden is light (Matt. 11:30).

I have discovered something wonderful about the Christian life. Jesus is not only good for the sweet by-and-by, but He is also good for the nasty here-and-now. He not only offers us the hope of heaven when we die, but He offers us help with our struggles on earth right now.

Here is one of the deep paradoxes of the Gospel. To people who were weighted down by life we would expect Jesus to say, "Follow Me and I will help you lay your burden down." But surprisingly He said, "Take My yoke upon you . . . and you will find rest." To those who were already wearied by the toils of life He offered the world's greatest symbol of toil.

Why does this work? It is because real peace and true rest are by-products of commitment. They are not to be sought directly, but they come ultimately as by-products of surrendering unreservedly to Jesus Christ. We are designed for obedience. We were created to do His will. When we follow Him in obedience it brings refreshing renewal to our minds (Rom. 12:1-2).

The yoke of Christ is well-fitted. The life Jesus gives us is not a burden that galls us. It is a joyous, victorious life. Whatever God leads us to do is fitted exactly to our abilities and needs. His will never chafes; it never galls.

Will you answer His great invitation and commit yourself to Christ today? When David Brainerd, a great missionary to the American Indians, was 17, he was confused about God's plan of salvation. He knew that the Bible told him to come to Christ, but he did not know how to come. He said, "I thought I would gladly come to Jesus, but I had no direction as to getting through."

As he prayed, Brainerd thought, "When a mother tells her child to come to her, she does not tell him how to come.

He may come with a run, a jump, a skip, or a leap. So, when a man comes to the Lord he may come praying, shouting, or singing, or even crying. It doesn't matter how he comes, so long as he comes."

This is God's great invitation to you. Come to Him—take His yoke upon you—learn of Him—and you will find the abundant life (John 10:10). Will you commit yourself to Him now?

2

Called to Humility

The worst "ism" facing our nation is not Communism, or liberalism, or racism, or materialism, but egotism.

Pride is one of the greatest and most common of all sins. It is the sin that made the devil into a devil. Satan was expelled from heaven, not because he got drunk or engaged in some form of immorality, but rather because he said in his heart, "I will exalt my throne above the stars of God; I will sit also upon the mount of the congregation . . . I will ascend above the heights of the clouds; I will be like the Most High" (Isa. 14:13-14). Because Satan sought to exalt himself above God, he was cast down. Pride was his downfall and it can be ours also.

Blaise Pascal said, "There are two kinds of men: the righteous who believe themselves to be sinners; the rest sinners who believe themselves to be righteous." That's why the Bible speaks so often about the sin of pride. Solomon listed seven deadly sins. The first one of these was pride (Prov. 6:16-19).

After King David's great sin, he made an agonizing confession to God. In that confession he said, "For Thou desirest not sacrifice; else I would give it. Thou delightest not in burnt offering. The sacrifices of God are a broken spirit; a broken and contrite heart, O God, Thou wilt not despise" (Ps. 51:16-17).

The Lord Jesus said, in His Sermon on the Mount, "Blessed are the poor in spirit, for theirs is the kingdom of heaven" (Matt. 5:3). And the Apostle Paul wrote, "For by grace are ye saved through faith; and that not of yourselves; it is the gift of God; not of works, lest any man should boast" (Eph. 2:8-9).

Have you ever wondered why God made salvation a matter of grace alone? He did it so we couldn't become proud over it. God could have allowed us to work for our salvation. He could have permitted us to earn our way to heaven. But if He had, we would promptly begin bragging about it. Thus, we would become worse in the end than we were in the beginning. So God made salvation completely of grace "lest any man should boast."

Jesus' call to commitment is a call to humility—the kind of humility that leads us to recognize our sins and to repent of them. It is a call to put aside all self-effort and self-righteousness and trust Christ completely for our salvation.

Webster talks about two kinds of pride: (1) "Pride may be commendatory in indicating a justified self-esteem, proper self-respect, or dislike of falling below one's standards that spurs one on, buoys one up, or checks one from base decisions." This kind of pride is a virtue. It is commendable. We would all be worse off without it. It makes a person want to do his best, look his best, and be his best. So far as I know the Bible never deals with this kind of pride.

But there's another kind of pride, which the Scriptures often attack. Going back to Webster, pride may be (2) "an unjustified self-esteem, arising from a false, inflated, and pretentious sense of one's worth, culminating in arrogant conceit." This kind of pride is contemptible. It is the kind of pride which makes us feel self-sufficient before God and superior to other people.

This parable of Jesus, about a Pharisee and a publican (Luke 18:9-14), deals with this second kind of pride. Luke tells us that Jesus spoke this parable to those people who "trusted in themselves that they were righteous and despised others" (18:9). Sinful pride always expresses itself in two directions—vertically and horizontally. In relationship to God it makes us feel independent and self-sufficient. We think that we are righteous within ourselves and we do not need God's help. In relationship to our fellowman, pride makes us feel superior. The word *despised* (18:9) means "to think nothing of." If we are proud, we do not value other people. We look down on them and they mean nothing to us. Pride causes us to strut in the presence of God and to look down our noses at other people.

Jesus illustrates what He is talking about by telling the story of two men who went to the temple one day to pray. One was a Pharisee; the other was a publican. These two men depict two opposite attitudes toward life. One is proud and self-righteous. The other is humble and repentant. The Pharisee was a superreligious person. He devoted his life to the study and keeping of God's Law. And as is the case with most legalists, the Pharisee's religion led to spiritual arrogance. He kept the letter of the Old Testament Law with exactness but missed the spirit of it. No one could fault his actions, but his attitude was horrible. He became proud, pompous, and self-righteous.

On the other hand, the publican was a tax collector. Israel was occupied territory. It had been conquered by Rome. Wherever Rome ruled, it taxed the people heavily. The Roman system of taxation was very simple, but it led to great corruption. A province would be farmed out by the government to a certain tax collector for a certain round net sum. He in turn farmed out the cities and towns to other tax collectors, for varying sums, depending on their population and wealth. Each tax collector turned in to the government the amount required, but he was allowed to keep for himself all the surplus he could get. So tax collectors were generally rich, corrupt, and hated. The worst of men sought these jobs and the jobs made them into still worse men.

More than that, they were traitors against their own people. They had gone over to the side of Israel's enemy and were working for them. Naturally they were among the most hated and despised people in their society.

So the Pharisee and the publican showed up in church on the same day. The Pharisee stood and prayed, "God, I thank Thee that I am not as other men are, extortioners, unjust, adulterers, or even as this publican. I fast twice in the week; I give tithes of all that I possess" (18:11-12).

This was really not a prayer; it was a testimonial. The Pharisee was saying, "God, I thank You for me. God, I know You must get discouraged when You look around at sinful humanity, but cheer up, God. Look at me! I am not like other men." With that he boasted of the evil that he did not do and the religious things that he did do.

The publican had an entirely different attitude. He found a seat as far in the back of the church as possible. He was obviously uncomfortable. He looked on the church as a place for good people to go. He wasn't good and he knew it. He was so ashamed of himself that he could not even lift up his face to heaven. So, with his head bowed, he prayed, "God, be merciful to me, a sinner." The article "a" in the Greek is the definite article. The publican was not simply confessing that he was "a sinner." He was really saying, "Have mercy on me, *the* sinner." He probably meant that he was the very sinner mentioned by the Pharisee.

Then came Jesus' evaluation of the two worship experiences. He said, "I tell you, this man [the publican] went down to his house justified rather than the other; for everyone that exalteth himself shall be abased; and he that humbleth himself shall be exalted" (18:14).

There is no more perilous sin than pride. Jesus said three things about it that we need to remember:

The Worst of Vices

First, *pride is the worst of all vices*. It is the king of sins. In his prayer the Pharisee thanked God that he was not like other men. Then he listed a trinity of evil that was not found in his life: extortion, injustice, and adultery. Look at this list for a moment.

He begins by saying he was not an extortioner. The word *extort* means to "snatch away, to steal, to take by force." Extortion describes that greedy, grasping spirit that will go to any length to get what it wants. It will cause a person to lie, to cheat, to steal, and to take advantage of the weaknesses of others for its own gain. The Bible warns us, "Hell and destruction are never full; so the eyes of man are never satisfied" (Prov. 27:20). Extortion tells us that the love of money is the root of all evil (1 Tim. 6:10). There is enough in the world for everybody's needs, but there is not enough for everybody's greeds. So some people stoop to extortion to get what they want.

Then, he said, he was not unjust. The word *unjust* is a comprehensive word for wrongdoing among people. It literally means to be unrighteous and wicked. Probably in this context it referred to the dishonesty of the tax collector. He had made himself rich at the expense of others. Many times, no doubt, he had taken the only ox or donkey of some poor farmer and had bodily taken away the furniture from some poor widow. And he had done it all in the name of the law.

There is a sense of justice in every one of us. When we are wronged, we cry out, "That's not fair!" It is a tragic thing when that sense of justice dies in us.

Then the Pharisee said that he was not an *adulterer.* God said, in the Ten Commandments, "Thou shalt not commit adultery" (Ex. 20:14). Repeatedly in the Bible we are warned against sexual immorality. Adultery has always been considered one of the worst of sins. Marriage is the cornerstone of our society. Adultery is the one thing that Jesus said can break the bonds of marriage. This makes adultery a great sin.

All of these things violate the basic Laws of God. They each break at least one of the Ten Commandments. Could anything be worse than this trinity of evil? Yes, one thing:

pride! Pride exceeds all other sins. It leads to comparisons and a feeling of superiority. It keeps us from repenting of the other sins that are in our lives. One kind of person who is worse than extortioners, unjust people, and adulterers is a person who looks down on them and feels superior to them.

Thomas Carlyle said, "The greatest of all sins is to be conscious of none." The proud man had no consciousness of sin and so he never repented and prayed, "God, be merciful to me, a sinner." The extortioner, the unjust, and the adulterer may recognize their sins and cry out to God for mercy. When they do, mercy and forgiveness are given. But a proud person never cries for help and thus he is never forgiven.

This parable forces us to reexamine our estimation of sin. The greatest of all sins is to believe that you are righteous in yourself. It is the greatest of all sins because it covers and excuses all your other sins. Pride leaves no room for repentance which God so greatly desires and demands. It feels no need of mercy which God is so willing to give. It is the most dangerous of sins because it is the one sin least likely to be confessed and forsaken.

Virtues Nullified

Second, *pride cancels out all of the other virtues in a person's life*. Not only did the Pharisee abstain from evil, but he also had many positive virtues in his life.

For one thing, he attended church. As the Scriptures say, he "went into the temple . . . " That's commendable. The Bible teaches that we should all be faithful in worship. It says that we should not forsake the assembling of ourselves together (Heb. 10:25).

T.S. Eliot said that when he flew across the Atlantic he lost three days waiting for his soul to catch up with his body. In this busy, hectic world in which we live it is so easy for us to outrun our souls. Worship is the pause that allows our souls to catch up. In worship we are confronted with God's scale of values, and we are given a sense of direction and we experience His source of power that helps us keep life in balance. We ought to be regular in church attendance, though we can also worship God elsewhere.

The Pharisee was also a man of prayer. In fact, this parable records his prayer. Nothing is more important in a Christian's life than prayer. Jesus preceded this parable with another parable which teaches us that "men ought always to pray and not to faint" (Luke 18:1). Sometimes these are the only two alternatives in life—praying or fainting. We are either sustained by God through prayer or we collapse under the pressure of life. Many turn to drugs and suicide as an escape from their pressures. But remember, if we hem up both ends of a day with prayer, it is not as likely to unravel in the middle. Prayer is the breath of the newborn soul, and there can be no Christian life without it. As every relationship is sustained by communication, so our relationship with God is sustained through prayer. We ought to pray, often.

The Pharisee also fasted. Fasting is the practice of abstaining from food for a period of time as an act of religious discipline and devotion. Fasting was commanded in the Old Testament, and was practiced by Jesus (Matt. 4:2) and by the Apostle Paul (2 Cor. 6:5; 11:27). It has both physical and spiritual benefits.

The Pharisee in our parable was also a tither. He gave tithes of "all" that he possessed. That means that he gave 10 percent of his possessions to God's work. You must have seen bumper stickers that say, "Honk if you love Jesus." I saw one the other day that said, "If you love Jesus, tithe. Anyone can honk." Tithing should be a part of your spiritual life.

Tithing has a long history. Abraham commenced it. Moses commanded it. Jesus commended it. So I am not about to cancel it. God loves a generous heart, for it is a heart akin to His.

All of these acts of the Pharisee were commendable. But because they became a point of pride their value was nullified. As Thomas á Becket is reported to have said, "What is life's greatest treason? But to do the right thing for the wrong reason." So, regardless of all the other virtues in our lives, we must add humility. Without humility we nullify all the other good we may do. Without humility we become worse in spirit than others are in practice. We may also become worse in attitude than others are in their actions.

We are never through with pride. It is so subtle that if we aren't careful we'll become proud of our humility. When this happens our goodness becomes badness. Our virtues become vices. We can easily become like the Sunday School teacher who, having told the story of the Pharisee and the publican, said, "Now, children, let's bow our heads and thank God that we are not like the Pharisee."

The Victory Lost

Finally, when Jesus evaluated these two men, He said concerning the publican, "this man went down to his house justified rather than the other" man (Luke 18:14). It was *pride* that *prevented the Pharisee from going down to his house justified.* He went home dignified but not justified.

Justification is the greatest and most important doctrine in the Bible. It means to be put right with the Law. It means to be acquitted, to be found not guilty. In the Christian sense, it means that through the work of Jesus Christ I as a believer become "just-as-if-I'd" never sinned. It means that I am forgiven, cleansed, and acceptable in God's sight.

But Jesus not only gave us an illustration of pride. He also gave us two examples of humility. In addition to telling us about the humble publican, Jesus set a little child on His knee and said, "Whosoever shall not receive the kingdom of God as a little child shall in no wise enter therein" (18:17). Jesus used the honesty, openness, and sincerity of a little child as an example for those who would enter the kingdom of heaven.

We must come to God with the same kind of honesty, openness, and humility if we expect to be a part of the kingdom of God. There is no other way to become right with God except through confession and trust in His Son. Pride blinds our eyes and prevents this kind of honesty and openness. If we let it, pride will shut up the gates of heaven to us.

Dr. R.A. Torrey once preached on the Parable of the Pharisee and the Publican and labeled it "the story of a good man lost and a bad man saved." His title is as fitting as it is striking, for that is exactly what happened. That is why we say that pride is the greatest of all sins. It keeps us from coming to God for mercy and forgiveness.

Mahatma Gandhi asked three missionaries who visited him during one of his numerous fasts to sing a hymn for him. "Which one?" they inquired. "The one that expresses all that is deepest in your faith," he replied. They thought for a moment and then with full hearts sang:

> When I survey the wondrous cross,
> On which the Prince of glory died,
> My richest gain I count but loss,
> And pour contempt on all my pride.

When we look at the cross, there is no place for pride, only the humility of the publican who said, "God, be merciful to me, a sinner." It is with this humility that we come to Christ. It is in this spirit that we continue to walk with Him day by day. His call to commitment is a call to this kind of humility and repentance.

3

Called to Childlikeness

Ever since Jesus came into the world it has been a better place for almost everyone, especially for the weak, the poor, and the helpless. The world before Jesus came was unbelievably cruel to such people. Most people, including slaves, women, and children, had almost no rights. They were more often treated as property than as people. Children especially were held in low esteem in the first century world. They were seldom seen with adults outside the home, and they were never to be heard from.

Into that kind of world Jesus came, saying that all people are valuable to God. Sinners, slaves, women, and children are just as important to Him as are kings and presidents. They are all made in God's image and they all are the objects of His love.

One day some parents brought their little children to Jesus so He would bless them. His disciples, seeking to protect Him, rebuked these parents. When Jesus saw what His disciples were doing, He was greatly displeased with them. He told them to allow the little children to come unto Him. "For," He said, "of such is the kingdom of God" (Mark 10:14). Then Jesus warned that if we do not receive the kingdom of God as a little child we "shall not enter therein."

The teaching of this passage is so important that it bears our careful investigation. The Greek word Mark uses for "children" indicates that these were not infants. They were children from 4 to 12 years of age. Their parents brought them to Jesus so that He would "touch" them. This alludes to the Old Testament practice of bringing children to a rabbi or a teacher that he might bless them. They believed that such a blessing was much more than just words, that it had power and affected the life of the person who was blessed. And the closer a teacher was to God, the more likelihood there was of his blessing's effectiveness. We can see why these parents were bringing their children to Jesus. They believed that Jesus walked with God as did no other man they knew. They were confident that His blessings would have a powerful effect on the lives of their children. So they brought them to Jesus in order that He would put His hands on them and bless them.

But the disciples "rebuked" those parents who brought their children to Jesus. There were two reasons why the disciples reacted as they did. First, Jesus was on His way to the cross. He had many things on His mind. They were probably trying to protect Him. They did not want Him to be bothered by unnecessary activity at this crucial time in His life. Then too, they probably held the low view of children that was prevalent in their day. Such an important person as Jesus could not be expected to waste His time with mere children. As far as the disciples were concerned children had nothing to contribute to the establishment of the kind of kingdom they had in mind.

When Jesus saw this, He was much displeased. The word *displeased* is a strong word. It expresses deep emotion. It means to be moved with indignation. It is the same word that was used when the chief priests and scribes were "sore displeased" at the people in the temple, who were crying, "Hosanna to the Son of David" (Matt. 21:15).

Then Jesus said to His disciples, "Suffer [allow] the little children to come unto Me and forbid them not, for of such is the kingdom of God" (Mark 10:14).

Jesus then chose this occasion to teach people about His kingdom. Using these little children as models, He said, "Verily I say unto you, whosoever shall not receive the kingdom of God as a little child, he shall not enter therein" (10:15). In the Greek Jesus used a double negative. Literally He said, "Whosoever shall not receive the kingdom of God as a little child *shall not never enter therein.*" That's not good English, but it is excellent Greek. It is the strongest possible way of saying something. Jesus was teaching us that if a person does not come to Him as a little child there is no possible way of his entering into the kingdom of God. Then Jesus took these children in His arms, put His hands on them, and blessed them.

This passage teaches us many things. First, it teaches us something about Jesus. It teaches us that Jesus must have been a joyful and winsome person. Neither parents nor children are attracted to a grouch. Children are keen detectors of character. They would not have been drawn to Jesus if He had not been loving and kind. It tells us that Jesus loved people, and in particular He loved little children.

George McDonald said, "I do not have faith in any man's Christianity if children are not found occasionally playing at his door." With all of His burdens and responsibilities, Jesus still had time for little children.

Second, the passage teaches us something about little children. They can and should be brought to Jesus. We need today an adequate theology concerning children. The question of the place of children in the kingdom of God and in the church is one which continually troubles some people. How are we to regard little children? Are they lost? Saved? Are they heathen? Potential converts? Christians? Are they the children of God or the children of wrath?

Jesus taught us that children can and should be brought to Him. Children are not born guilty of sin but with a sinful nature. As they grow that nature reveals itself by rebellion against authority, including God's. When they are old enough to be aware of God and conscious of sinning against Him, they should be led to trust Jesus as their Saviour. Children can and will believe in Christ if given an opportunity. That's why Jesus tells us to do nothing to hinder them from coming to Him or being brought to Him.

Third, this passage teaches us about the kingdom of God. Jesus chose this occasion to use children as a model for those who would enter into the kingdom of God. There is no possible way for anyone to enter into the kingdom of God without having the spirit, attitude, and disposition of a little child. Christ's call to commitment is a call then to childlikeness. It is a call to come to Him and trust in Him with the same open spirit and trusting attitude that a little child has.

What is there about little children that we need, in order to enter into the kingdom of heaven?

Little Children Are Honest

One of the things that characterizes *little children* is that they *have not yet learned to cover up their feelings.* How early we learn to put on a facade and cover up our true feelings. But children are nearly always honest and open. They have not yet developed the kind of pride, pretense, and deception that causes adults to mask their true feelings.

Art Linkletter capitalized on this characteristic. He used to put children on television, ask them leading questions, and they told everything. He wrote some of his questions and their answers in his book *Kids Say the Darnedest Things.* It is wonderful and refreshing to be around children.

Years ago I returned to a former pastorate to conduct revival meetings. One of the delightful experiences that happened to me that week was with a small 10-year-old boy who made his profession of faith. I had baptized his brother years earlier and his parents wanted me to baptize him also. Later that week I did. During the week Bret and I became close friends. Everywhere I went, he went. He was always on my coattail, always talking to me. When the last service was over, I asked him to go with me to my room and help me pack. When we were through, I gave him a bag of fruit that a friend had given me earlier that week. That made him happy. Then I took him home. Three days later I received this letter from him:

> Dear Bro. Powell:
> I like the fruit that you gave me. You are the best person that I ever knew. I have fun with you. I will come to see you. I like you. Do you like me? Answer yes or no. Come and see me sometimes. I like you very much. This summer we will see you. By the way, could you pay me for helping you?
> Love,
Bret

That's honesty! That's openness! "Do you like me? Answer yes or no!" No ifs, ands, or buts about it. Just a straightforward question. There is something about the honesty and openness of a child that intrigues all of us.

If you want to get into the kingdom of God, you must have that kind of honesty and openness. You must stop covering up your feelings. You must stop playacting with God. You must stop pretending. You must be honest enough to confess you are a sinner, repent of your sins, and trust your life to Christ. That is what Jesus meant when He said, "Except ye be converted, and become as little children, ye shall not enter into the kingdom of heaven" (Matt. 18:3).

Little Children Are Forgiving

Little children are forgiving to those who wrong them. They have not yet learned to hold grudges and resentments. Even after they are mistreated or abused, they have a marvelous capacity to forgive and to forget. It would take a calculator to count the number of times my two boys used to fight. But 15 minutes after a fight they had forgotten it and would be playing together again. I remember once they were fighting and I went into the room to discipline them. When I interrogated them, one of them said, "No, Dad, we weren't fighting. He's my buddy." That's typical of little children.

But as we grow older we learn to hold grudges and resentments. After someone wrongs us we may not ever forget it. Jesus taught us in the Lord's Prayer to pray "Forgive us our debts as we forgive our debtors" (Matt. 6:12). This is the only part of that prayer that Jesus amplified. He said that if we do not forgive other people for trespassing or sinning against us, then our heavenly Father will not forgive us for our trespasses (6:14-15).

It is as simple as that. A person who cannot forgive others destroys the bridge over which he himself must walk. We who belong to the kingdom of God must learn to forgive as little children do.

Little Children Are Responsive

Children are very responsive. Their hearts are soft and pliable. They have a spontaneity that enables them to act at once on what they understand. The impulse is not strangled by a calculated and cautious skepticism. Jesus welcomes spontaneous impulses, as Peter's confession (Matt. 16:15-17) and Mary's breaking of the alabaster box of precious ointment (John 12:3-8). This spirit is indispensable to the enterprise of His kingdom.

French statesman Talleyrand once said profoundly, even though cynically, "Distrust first impressions. They are nearly always right." True! It is the double-checking of our childlike spontaneity which has frustrated so much Christian movement. There is evangelical wisdom in the remark, "Don't look before you leap. If you do, you will decide to sit down." We need the mind of a little child in order to respond quickly to what our hearts feel.

The older we get, the harder and the more calloused our hearts become. And the less likely we are to respond to God. You might think that the more people sin, the more conscious they would become of the sin in their lives. But the opposite is true. The more we sin, the less aware we become of sin. Sin has a way of numbing our consciences. Hosea said, "Whoredom and wine and new wine take away the heart" (Hosea 4:11). Or "Wine, women, and song have robbed My people of their brains" (LB).

The Amplified Bible puts it, "Harlotry and wine and new wine take away the heart and the mind [and spiritual] understanding." That's the way sin is. It breaks down our moral resistance and dulls our understanding so that we do not respond to God as we ought. We who belong to the kingdom of God must become as little children in our responsiveness to Him. When He calls us we must respond and yield ourselves to Him wholeheartedly.

Little Children Believe

One of the most characteristic marks of little children is that they live by faith. They live in total dependence on others for nearly everything. They do not worry or become anxious about anything. If grocery prices spiral, they do not worry. If we are facing an energy crisis, they are not anxious. They look to their parents for all of their needs.

We must also become like little children in our faith and trust. There is a time when a child thinks that his father knows everything and that his father is always right. In a few years he outgrows this. But even after that a child who gets in trouble instinctively realizes his own ignorance and helplessness and trusts the one who, he thinks, knows what to do.

Little children trust everybody. They trust their neighbors. They trust their teachers. They trust strangers. In fact, you have to caution them about being too trusting. You have to warn them not to get into cars with strangers. They tend to trust everybody.

To enter into the kingdom of God, we must come to Christ with this kind of faith in Him. We must come to God in total, absolute trust. Anyone who tries to get into God's kingdom on the basis of his own self-worth, position, or power will find the way to eternal life barred to him. Children possess neither the power nor the might to do much of anything for themselves. That's the kind of person to whom the kingdom of God is given.

Faith is so simple that it is elusive. We are familiar with John 3:16: "For God so loved the world, that He gave His only begotten Son, that whosoever believeth in Him should not perish, but have everlasting life." And when we have finished saying it we feel that we ought to add something to it. We think it needs to be explained. But it is enough. It really is as simple as that. The problem is not with John 3:16. The problem is with our ability to trust God and His Son.

We do not enter into the kingdom of God as Ph.Ds. We enter in as little children. We do not understand everything, but we can trust our heavenly Father. If we can believe in Jesus Christ as our Saviour and Lord we can enter into God's kingdom. The kingdom does not belong to the mighty, to the strong, to the influential. It belongs to the weak, to the insignificant, and to the helpless.

What does it mean to become as a little child? It means to be open and honest with God and ourselves. It means to forgive so that we can be forgiven. It means to respond to the call of God. It means to trust in God fully and completely.

Perhaps you had a similar experience as a child. It was the middle of the night and you cried out, "Mother, Mother, it's so dark and I'm so afraid. Take my hand."

So we say to God:

Precious Lord, take my hand.
Lead me on, let me stand.
I am tired, I am weak, I am worn.
Through the storm, through the night,
Lead me on to the light.
Precious Lord, take my hand,
Lead me home.

When we have enough faith, like a little child, to reach up to God and say "Lord, take my hand," He does the rest.

4

Called to Sincerity

Ours is an age of imitations, veneers, and camouflages. Pretense has never stood in so eminent a position as it does today. If you walk down the main streets of most of our cities and look at the buildings, you would probably think that they are fairly new. Actually, many are very old structures with new faces. A thin veneer of brick, metal, or stone only makes them appear new and up-to-date. Our modern use of wood veneers, artificial flowers, and cosmetics is a part of everyday life.

Have you ever thought of how many different things a woman can do to change her hair? She can cut it, curl it, tease it, tint it, frost it, or dye it. Then if she still doesn't like it, she can cover it with a wig. Some women have so many ways to camouflage themselves that you seldom know what they really look like. Some of them remind me of the lady who along with her husband was gardening one Saturday afternoon when a moving van arrived next door. They hastened over in their work clothes to greet their new neighbors.

The following week the new neighbors invited them to a housewarming party. As they dressed, the lady's husband watched in fascination as she added a fall to her hair, struggled into a girdle, painted her lips, applied eye shadow and false eyelashes, enameled her fingernails, and popped in her contact lenses. Finally, she looked into the mirror and said with a satisfied sigh, "Well, tonight they are going to see the real me!"

Of course there is nothing wrong with wood veneers, artificial flowers, or cosmetics. But it is a tragedy when people camouflage their characters or coat their lives with a thin veneer of religion and become artificial. Many people are religious counterfeits. They are impostors, phonies, pretenders. They are hypocrites.

Christ's call to commitment is a call to sincerity in our Christian profession. It is a call to put away all sham and pretense and to be genuine, honest, and real in our commitment. He makes this clear when He warns, "Beware ye of the leaven of the Pharisees, which is hypocrisy. For there is nothing covered, that shall not be revealed; neither hid, that shall not be known. Therefore, whatsoever ye have spoken in darkness shall be heard in the light; and that which ye have spoken in the ear in closets shall be proclaimed upon the housetops" (Luke 12:1-3).

What or who is a hypocrite? We need to know. Our churches are constantly being accused of being full of them. Jesus answers this question when He tells us to beware of the leaven (influence or spirit) of the Pharisees, which is hypocrisy.

We can best learn what a hypocrite is by looking at the Pharisees. They are classic examples of what we should not be. As a group the Pharisees put a strong emphasis on the externals of religion and neglected the inward parts. They were concerned about appearances but lacked spiritual sincerity. They drew near to God with their lips but their hearts were far from Him. Their religion depended on time and place. When they were at God's house they were pious and holy. When they were elsewhere they were evil and heartless. They were careful to give tithes of all they possessed on the Sabbath, but they were crooked in their business dealings during the week. Their religion did not affect their daily lives. Jesus said that this is hypocrisy.

The word *hypocrite* originally came from the field of drama in the days when one person played several parts in a play. The actor wore a different mask for each character he portrayed. In one scene he might be the villain. In the next scene he might be the hero. He simply put on a different mask for each character. Such a person was called a hypocrite. The word had a good meaning at first, but gradually it came to describe a person who was two-faced, one who was playacting or pretending in real life.

A religious hypocrite is one who is playacting or two-faced in religion. He may be regular in church attendance, diligent in Bible study, generous in his giving, but in his business and at home he is altogether different. He may be unjust, dishonest, cruel, ill-tempered, or profane. He is not sincere or consistent.

But don't be confused. Not all who fail to live up to their profession of faith are hypocrites. Many people are sincere in their desire to live for God but fail due to weakness or temptation. The difference between a weak Christian and a hypocrite is intent. A genuine Christian is sincere in his desire to live for God. A hypocrite is concerned only with appearances. He is just playacting in his religious profession.

True commitment makes us sincere and genuine followers of Christ. In this teaching Jesus tells us three things about hypocrisy that will help us guard against it.

No One Is Immune

Jesus began His teaching with the warning "Beware . . . of . . . hypocrisy" (Luke 12:1). If ever there was a time when we needed to keep our guard up against hypocrisy, it is now.

A minister may not have to preach this doctrine in times of persecution. For suffering is a keen detector of impostors.

In Russia, for example, there is no need to preach on hypocrisy. A recent newspaper article dealing with religion in Russia today pointed out why this is true. It said that despite the fact that atheism has been the official teaching of Communism for almost 50 years and there are no laws against going to church or believing in God in the Soviet Union, it still takes a great deal of devotion and often guts to practice one's faith. For example, during Easter season services, priests and communicants are often jeered as they enter churches, and occasionally hooligans try to molest them. The article also pointed out how workers at a certain cardboard box factory tried their best through argument and insult to turn their plant into a closed shop for atheism.

They "persuaded" several co-workers to "give up" their belief in God. And when jeers and catcalls failed to persuade two other believers to "see the light" they were taunted with dirty stories and intimidated in other ways.

Such sledgehammer tactics have a way of eliminating hypocrisy. But in our land religion is more respectable. It is popular to follow Christ for business and social reasons. So today we need to be warned again and again: "Beware . . . of . . . hypocrisy."

Sincerity never comes easily or automatically. Francois de la Rochefoucauld was right in saying, "Sincerity is an openness of heart; we find it in very few people." Elizabeth Christman expressed the same idea: "Young people prize sincerity above almost any other quality. One of their most frequent complaints against adults is that they are phony. But sincerity is not an easy matter to achieve, and conscious attitudes are not necessarily real attitudes. The greatest liars often consider themselves sincere because they are completely successful in lying to themselves."

There is some hypocrisy in all of us. A man's conduct is generally little better than his heart. Shakespeare said, "All the world's a stage, and all the men and women merely players! They have their exits and their entrances; and one man in his time plays many parts." We all put on Oscar-winning performances at times.

In 1886 Robert Louis Stevenson wrote the story of Dr.

Jekyll and Mr. Hyde. The handsome, kindly Dr. Jekyll discovered a drug that had the supernatural power to change his personality. He tasted the potent liquid and immediately was transformed into the misshapen monster Mr. Hyde, whose only delight was in evil deeds. So he lived for many years as two people. At times he was the kind and gentle Dr. Jekyll, and at times he became the evil and sinister Mr. Hyde. He worked the transformation many times. But at last the drug lost its magic and the monstrous Mr. Hyde, unable ever again to be Dr. Jekyll, killed himself in despair.

The tragedy is that not all Dr. Jekylls and Mr. Hydes are in fiction. Some of them are with us today. Some of us are living a double life. We are two-faced Jekyll-and-Hyde personalities. You may be a young person who at home pretends to be clean and wholesome. But away from home you are profane and filthy-minded. You may be a woman who is an angel at church but a devil at home. At church your lips drip with honey but at home they reek with venom. You may be a person who says beautiful prayers at church, while outside the church you carry on an extramarital affair. Or maybe you are dishonest in your business.

The danger of playacting and insincerity faces all of us, constantly. Remember that Judas was among the 12. We all ought to pray daily, "O God, make me sincere and make me consistent."

A Sin of the Worst Kind

Most people are continually trying to label sins as little sins or big sins. The Bible never does that. *To God, all sins are big.* The Bible tells us, "All have sinned, and come short of the glory of God" (Rom. 3:23). The so-called big sins are deadly but so are the so-called little sins.

Dr. W.W. Melton, former Texas Baptist leader, once told a story about enjoying rattlesnake hunting in his youth. One day he and an older friend were out hunting and he heard a snake rattling in the weeds. By its sound he knew it was just a small snake. So he bravely walked out in the grass to find it.

His older friend cautioned him about his carelessness. Melton replied that his friend needn't worry; it was only a small one. But his friend reminded him that it was enough that it was a rattlesnake. Then Melton said he remembered that a little rattlesnake can kill you just as dead as a big one. It has all the poison and venom necessary for death.

Just so, all sins, big and little, are deadly. But if we go to the Bible we see that Jesus denounced some sins more severely than others. The sins He singled out were not murder or adultery or stealing. They were pride (looking down your nose at others), indifference (seeing a need and not acting), and especially hypocrisy.

Hypocrisy is the sin that Jesus condemned most scathingly. It seems that to Him there was nothing worse than a religious phony. His most biting indictments were *not* against the moral degenerates, the traitors, the prostitutes, the adulterers, the thieves, or the murderers. They were against religious phonies. He brought His most caustic judgment down on those who refused to face the truth about themselves.

Jesus was and is the sinner's friend. In fact Jesus received His most severe criticism from the religious leaders of His day because He welcomed sinners as His friends and even went so far as to eat with them (Mark 2:16; Luke 15:2). But the religious leaders of Jesus' day were sinfully exclusive. They had nothing to do with moral degenerates, social outcasts, and those who did not live by their ceremonial law. Jesus, on the other hand, loved all people and even called the hated and despised tax collector Matthew to be His disciple.

At the city water well of Sychar, He violated the social and religious tradition of His day by conversing with the town tramp. This woman had been married five times and was now living with a man who was not her husband. But Jesus accepted her, loved her, and redeemed her.

Jesus had a logical explanation for mixing and mingling with the masses. He told His critics that well people do not need a doctor. Hospitals are not built for the healthy. It is the sick who need medical care. And a doctor cannot properly diagnose an illness or prescribe a cure without contact with his patients. A physician who is so afraid of contamination that he avoids contact with the sick can never be effective (Mark 2:17).

Don't get the wrong impression. Jesus certainly did not condone people's sinfulness. He came to call sinners to repentance. He expected them to make a complete spiritual about-face, believe in Him, and turn from their sins. But He knew that it was only through love, acceptance, and contact with people that He could ever lead them to repentance. So, what His critics intended as a jibe became Jesus' crowning glory, "This man welcomes sinners and eats with them."

If you are a sinner and know it, Jesus is your friend. But He has no use for a hypocrite until he gives up his pretense. God help all of us face the truth about ourselves. He would rather that you be a blatant, honest sinner than someone who puts on an act of goodness and is not sincere. Let there be no pretense about you. Be sincere, genuine, and consistent.

You Can't Get Away with It

Jesus pointed out the futility of hypocrisy when He said, "For there is nothing covered, that shall not be revealed; neither hid, that shall not be known. Therefore, whatsoever ye have spoken in darkness shall be heard in the light; and that which ye have spoken in the ear in closets shall be proclaimed upon the housetops" (Luke 12:2-3).

Someday we shall all be revealed for what we really are. *We can't fool God.* We may fool our friends. We may fool the preacher. And we may even fool our family. But we can't fool God. One day our long-buried sins will be uncovered and our hidden secrets will be made known. "Be sure your sin will find you out," the Bible warns (Num. 32:23).

When I was a boy I had a job delivering advertising circulars. The boss would drop me off at the end of a street with a large bundle of circulars and I was to zigzag back and forth across the street, placing advertisements in the screen door of each home.

One day when it was especially hot and I was tired, I decided to cheat a little. I dropped a large bundle of circulars down a storm drain, and then strolled casually down the street, confident that no one would ever know the difference.

A few days later it began to rain. And wouldn't you know it— that storm drain stopped up. So the city sanitation crew was called out to unstop it. Amid the sticks and wire in that drain they found hundreds of circulars. Naturally it was reported to my boss.

He called me in and said, "Paul, I won't mind losing the circulars so much if you'll just learn a lesson: 'Be sure your sin will find you out.'"

The verse does not say, "Be sure your sin will be found out." It says, "Be sure your sin will find *you* out." It will catch up with you and you will have to pay for it. I learned my lesson that day.

How often the Scriptures remind us of the searching, scrutinizing eye of the Lord. "For the eyes of the Lord run to and fro throughout the whole earth, to show Himself strong in behalf of them whose heart is perfect toward Him" (2 Chron. 16:9).

Psalmist Moses wrote, "Thou hast set our iniquities before Thee, our secret sins in the light of Thy countenance" (Ps. 90:8).

Solomon wrote, "The eyes of the Lord are in every place, beholding the evil and the good" (Prov. 15:3). Solomon also wrote, "For God shall bring every work into judgment, with every secret thing, whether it be good or whether it be evil" (Ecc. 12:14).

The Prophet Jeremiah quoted God: "For Mine eyes are upon all their ways: they are not hid from My face, neither is their iniquity hid from Mine eyes" (Jer. 16:17).

And the writer of Hebrews said, "Neither is there any

creature that is not manifest in His sight: but all things are naked and opened unto the eyes of Him with whom we have to do" (Heb. 4:13).

We dare not miss the cumulative witness of these verses. God sees and knows all. Eventually we will reap what we have sown. One day our sins will find us out.

Robert Louis Stevenson was right when he said, "Everybody, sooner or later, sits down to a banquet of consequences." If you are a hypocrite, you will be unmasked eventually. The veneer will one day be peeled away. The whitewash will be removed. Your only hope is to stop pretending and become sincere in your commitment now. Be honest with God. The prayer of every one of us must ever be, "O God, make me genuine."

For that's what a real Christian is—a sincere follower of Christ.

5

Called to Fellowship

In 1927 Charles Lindbergh made the first solo flight across the Atlantic. He traveled from New York City to Paris, France, a distance of over 3,600 miles. His speed was a phenomenal 108 miles per hour. The journey took him 33½ hours.

Recently the U.S. government revealed a strategic reconnaissance jet, the SR71. It made a similar journey from New York City to London, England, a distance of 3,460 miles. It took 1 hour and 56 minutes. The plane flew at an average speed of 1,800 miles an hour and sometimes at speeds of 2,000 miles an hour. It was flying faster than a 30.06 bullet does when it first leaves the barrel of a rifle.

We are all captivated by that kind of speed. That's because we are always in a hurry. We are always busy. Someone has said that our society could best be characterized by three words—Hurry! Worry! Bury! The modern American is pictured as a person running up an escalator.

There is nothing wrong with being busy. But there is a subtle danger associated with it. It is that we shall become so busy doing so many things that we have no time left for the most important things. There is a danger that we shall allow the pressing, the good, and the temporal things of life to crowd out those things that are most needful, the best, and the eternal. We may become so occupied with our jobs, social activities, recreation, and school that we not have time for the things we really need to do. We can even become so busy *for* God that we have no time to spend *with* Him.

Christ's call to commitment is therefore a call to the right priorities in life. It is a call not to become so busy working for the Lord that we neglect our devotional lives. It is a call to take time for fellowship with Him. Jesus taught us this on one of His visits with Mary, Martha, and Lazarus at their home in Bethany. As Jesus talked, Mary sat at His feet, listening to His words (Luke 10:39). To sit at someone's feet was an idiom in the New Testament world for being a disciple of, being a learner of, someone. Paul said that he sat at the feet of Gamaliel. This was the usual posture and the position of a disciple.

In contrast to Mary, Martha was "cumbered about much serving" (10:40). The word *cumbered* means to be distracted. It means to be drawn first in one direction and then in another. It means to be pulled this way and then to be pulled that way. It is the picture of a person who is anxious and uptight. Martha was so concerned about preparing a meal for Jesus that she became nervous and tense. She had obviously taken on more than she could handle. She was trying to be a good hostess, but everything needed to be done at once. She had no one to help her, so she became exasperated.

She expressed her irritation when she asked Jesus if He did not care that she had to do all of the serving alone. It didn't seem fair for her sister to sit around listening to Jesus talk when there was so much work to be done. So she urged Jesus to tell Mary to get up and help out in the kitchen.

Jesus said to her, "Martha, Martha, thou art careful and troubled about many things. But one thing is needful; and Mary hath chosen that good part, which shall not be taken from her" (10:41-42).

Martha had become so anxious over trying to prepare a meal for Jesus that her service to Jesus had become a source of irritation in her own life. Whenever that happens to us, something is wrong with our service. It has become self-defeating. We are either trying to do too much, or we are doing it in the wrong way. We need to back off and reexamine our lives.

Jesus told Martha that while she was trying to do "many things" Mary had chosen the "one thing" that was needful, good, and eternal.

This then is the peril of being too busy—we can become so involved in trying to do the many things that are pressing in on us that we neglect to do the one thing that is really most important. There is a continual struggle in our lives between the things that are best and the many things that are pressing. Discipleship demands that we establish priorities, recognize what is important, and choose correctly.

We can all identify with Martha. We too are busy people. However, Jesus' reply pointed out to her and to us the peril of being too busy.

In contrast, Jesus described what Mary was doing as needful, good, and eternal. What was it? It was spending time in fellowship with Him. It was listening to His words. It was being His disciple. The most important thing in all of life is our relationship with Him. Whatever else we do we must not cause our relationship with Him to be crowded out. We must not become so busy working *for* the Lord that we have no time to be *with* the Lord.

Our relationship with Him is established by faith and then maintained through a personal devotional life. In the midst of all the demands of life we must remember to keep our relationship with Christ up-to-date and in good repair.

It is no accident that this Mary and Martha episode follows the parable of the Good Samaritan. Jesus had just told the story of a man who busied himself with helping someone else. He closed that story by telling His disciples, "Go, and do thou likewise" (10:37). But lest we think that helping others is the sum total of Christianity, Jesus quickly warns us not to get too busy to spend time with Him. There should always be a balance in a Christian's life. Outer involvement cannot substitute for inner devotion. Our ministry must be balanced by meditation.

Like Mary and Martha we all face the choice between the many things that crowd into our lives and the thing that is needful. When Jesus said that what Mary was doing was needful, good, and eternal, He was pointing out to us the three dangers of being too busy:

The Pressing Can Crowd Out the Needful

The first peril of being too busy is that *the pressing tends to crowd out the needful*. We all know what it is to be pressed. There are a thousand things beckoning for our allegiance, our service, our devotion, and our time. There are causes, clubs, and organizations by the scores that bid for us.

And every one of these wants the first place in our lives. If we would allow it, every club, every cause, and every organization would dominate our time, our thinking, and our talents. Every cause wants to be the dominant cause in our lives. Every organization wants to be the most important organization in our lives. Every office wants to claim our supreme allegiance. It wants our best time, our greatest abilities, and our keenest interest. We find ourselves squeezed by many different interests that cry, "This needs to be done, this is pressing, this is vital." It is so easy to slip into that kind of situation, for it always happens gradually. We take on this responsibility, join that club, get involved in that project, and the first thing we know we are like a fly caught in a web. We become the victims of our own poor planning.

The best things in life do not crowd. Prayer never crowds out our TV time. Bible reading never crowds out the newspaper. And prayer meeting and visitation never crowd out recreation. The best things in life must be given priority. Otherwise they get crowded out all together. In this kind of world the serious disciple of Jesus is one who can discern between the pressing and the needful. Amid all the voices that call for his time, he says yes to the one supreme voice, the voice of his Master.

If you are busy climbing the ladder of success, you had better stop occasionally and check your priorities. If you don't, you may get to the top and discover that your ladder is leaning against the wrong wall. Obviously, there are many things in our lives that receive a large part of our time which are not worth a thing. So, if we are going to be true to Jesus and do all that we ought to do, then we must separate the many things that call to us from the one thing that is needful. All of our personal goals, ambitions, activities, and desires should be balanced with the one thing that is most important—our relationship with Him.

A man met a longtime friend on the street one day. He asked him, "Friend, how is it with your soul?"

The man replied, "You know, I've been so busy lately I had almost forgotten I have a soul."

This can happen to you. The many pressing things in your life can crowd out the one thing that is needful.

The Good Can Crowd Out the Best
Second, *the good things in life may crowd out the best.* Jesus said that Mary had chosen the good part. That word for *good* literally means "that which is of greatest value, that which is best."

Martha had lost her perspective. What she was doing was good and worthwhile, but she was missing the thing that was most important. She was so concerned about preparing physical bread that she had forgotten that man does not live by bread alone. She was neglecting the spiritual food that could sustain her inwardly. There is nothing wrong with wanting to be a good hostess. And there are far greater evils than being energetic, ambitious, and vivacious. But while such things may be good, they can be pursued to the exclusion of the best.

Our choices in life are not always between right and wrong, black and white, good and evil. Many times our choices are between the good and the best. Again we must have perception to be able to discern between the two.

Martha's problem was not in serving but in "much" serving. She was trying to do too much. Her problem was not her motive; it was her judgment. She had good intentions but poor priorities. She was spending all of her time on her feet cooking, when she needed to spend much of her time at His feet listening.

We cannot do everything. Therefore we must be selective, so that we do the best things. As life presses in on you, more and more you are going to have to choose between the good and the best if you are going to keep your relationship with Jesus alive. So the second danger of being too busy is that the good may crowd out the best.

The Temporal Can Crowd Out the Eternal

The third peril of being too busy is that *the temporal may crowd out the eternal*. Jesus said, "Mary has chosen that good part, which shall not be taken away from her" (10:42). What Mary had chosen was of eternal value. It would last forever. The meal would be enjoyable for a few minutes and sufficient for a few hours. Then they would all be hungry again and the whole process would have to be done over. But spiritual food keeps on sustaining us forever. It is like the fountain of living water that flows continually and satisfies eternally. When Jesus said that man does not live by bread alone (Matt. 4:4), He was not saying that bread was unimportant. He was saying that it is insufficient. We must have food. But there is something in us that meat and potatoes cannot satisfy. There is an eternal part of us that must not be neglected.

The Apostle Paul said, "Exercise thyself rather unto godliness. For bodily exercise profiteth little; but godliness is profitable unto all things, having promise of the life that now is, and of that which is to come" (1 Tim. 4:7-8). Paul was contrasting the value of spiritual exercise with bodily exercise. He did not say bodily exercise was unimportant. He only said that it is of limited value. It is helpful only as long as we live on this earth. However, spiritual exercise is of value both in this life and in the life to come. It is of eternal significance.

We must learn to distinguish between the temporal and the eternal. In Milan, Italy is a cathedral that has three front doors. Above the door on the left are inscribed these words, "All that pleases is but for a moment." Above the door on the right are chiseled these words, "All that troubles is but for a moment." Above the door in the middle are these words, "Only that which is eternal matters."

Material things are temporal. Jesus said, "Lay not up for yourselves treasures upon earth, where moth and rust doth corrupt, and where thieves break through and steal. But lay up for yourselves treasures in heaven, where neither moth nor rust doth corrupt, and where thieves do not break through nor steal" (Matt. 6:19-20). The Bible warns us that we brought nothing into this world and we shall take nothing out of it (1 Tim. 6:7). We are foolish then if we allow the material things of life to dominate our lives.

Pleasure is temporal, just temporary. The Bible tells us that by faith Moses, when he was come to years, "refused to be called the son of Pharaoh's daughter, choosing rather to suffer affliction with the people of God than to enjoy the pleasures of sin for a season" (Heb. 11:24-25). There is pleasure in sin. Even the Bible admits that. But it lasts only "for a season." The pleasure sin offers is temporary. But the joy of following the Lord is an eternal joy.

Esau made the mistake of giving in to his immediate desires and sold his spiritual birthright for a bowl of soup. Later he recognized his error and wept and repented, but what he had done could not be undone (Gen. 27:36-38; Heb. 12:16-17). The joys and pleasures of this world do not satisfy. They are joys but for a moment.

In his novel *Humboldt's Gift*, Paul Bellow described the

onset of fame: "I experienced the high voltage of publicity. It was like picking up a dangerous wire, fatal to ordinary folks. It was like the rattlesnakes handled by hillbillies in a state of religious exaltation." Some who grasp those charged serpents will themselves incandesce in the limelight for a little while and then wink out, like defunct flashlights, dead fireflies. Thus they will have obeyed Warhol's Law, first pronounced by Andy Warhol, the monsignor of transcience and junk culture: "In the future, everyone will be famous for at least 15 minutes."

Even religious success is temporal. The 70 missionaries Jesus had sent out came back rejoicing, because of the power He had given them. But Jesus told them, "In this rejoice not, that the spirits are subject unto you. But rather rejoice because your names are written in heaven" (Luke 10:17-20).

If we rejoice because evil spirits or something else is under our control, we are rejoicing in our success. However, the time will come when such things will not be subject unto us, when we will not be successful, when we will be failures. Then, if success was the reason for our happiness, we will be doomed to disappointment and despair.

But if our joy is in our relationship with Him and not in our success, that joy cannot be taken away. If we rejoice in the fact that our names are written in the Lamb's Book of Life, we will always have something to rejoice about. So we must not let even our service for the Lord interfere with our relationship with Him.

Jesus said that Mary had "chosen that good part." The choice was hers. That's the way it always is. The choice is always ours as to whether we will sit at Jesus' feet or will busy ourselves at many other things of lesser importance.

A thousand years ago some great saint of God said, "If you do not have a quiet time with God, it is not because you are too busy. It is because you don't care for Him."

Life has changed a great deal in the last 1,000 years. But it is still true that if you don't have a quiet time with God, it is not because you are too busy. It is because you don't care enough for Him. The choice was Mary's and Martha's. And the choice is ours.

The question we all face is this: Will we choose to be distracted by all that the world has to offer, or will we daily choose to sit at Jesus' feet as disciples, as learners, to listen to and obey Him?

Martin Luther said, "If I were the devil, I would not be one who decided against God, but one who in eternity came to no decision." That's the danger that we all face. Not that we who are Christians will purposely decide against God. We would never do that. But it's possible that we might never come to any decision at all. Many or most who claim to be Christians usually drift through life and allow the needful things, the best things, the eternal things to be pushed and crowded out, rather than choosing to put spiritual things first. The choice is yours. And the consequences are eternal.

6

Called to Excellence

A Washington lobbyist claimed that former President Gerald Ford was "superbly average." That's not the greatest of compliments. If you are average, half of the people are above you and half of the people are below you. You are right in the middle. That means that you are either the sorriest of the best or the best of the sorriest.

A lot of emphasis is given to the average person nowadays. Politicians aim their promises at the average American. Advertising is pitched at the average consumer. Entertainment is aimed at the average citizen. Not long ago education was geared to the average student, as not much adjusting was done for those above and below average. Some labor unions, allowed to go to extremes, tell workers to stop when they have done a certain amount of work. And promotions that are based on seniority alone tend to reduce everybody to average. Nobody excels. Even the government has done things which make people more average. If they take enough from the industrious in the form of taxes and give enough to the poor in the form of welfare, they are making people more financially average.

The humor of it all is that when we get sick we don't want an average doctor to attend us. When we need legal counsel, we don't want an average lawyer to represent us. When we are at war, we don't want an average general to lead us. And when we are looking for a college president, we don't want an average educator. In times of crisis, we don't want the common man—we want the *un*common man.

Though average people are plentiful, we should remind ourselves that the greatest strides in human progress have been made not by average people but by those who were above average. Take Abraham Lincoln and Thomas Edison, for example. Though both of them had humble origins, they overcame most of their difficulties. They both were men with superior ability and they both worked hard. They were uncommon men.

I share the feelings of Robert Frost, who wrote, "All men are born free and equal—free at least in their right to be different. Some people want to homogenize society everywhere. I'm against the homogenizers in art, in politics, in every walk of life. I want the cream to rise."

One pressing need of our world today is for more people to rise above the average—in business, in politics, in science, in education, and in the church.

This is one of Jesus' appeals. He wants His people to rise above the average. He wants us to be uncommon people. His call to commitment is a call to excellence. Jesus said, "Ye have heard it hath been said, Thou shalt love thy neighbor, and hate thine enemy. But I say unto you, Love your enemies, bless them that curse you, do good to them that hate you, and pray for them which despitefully use you, and persecute you; that ye may be the children of your Father which is in heaven: for He maketh His sun to rise on the evil and on the good, and sendeth rain on the just and on the unjust. For if ye love them which love you, what reward have ye? Do not even the publicans the same? And if ye salute your brethren only, *what do ye more than others?* Do not even the publicans so? Be ye therefore perfect, even as your Father which is in heaven is perfect" (Matt. 5:43-48).

When Jesus asked, "What do ye more than others?" He

was challenging us to rise above the average. That little word *more* spotlights Christian excellence. We need to lodge that question in our minds and apply it to all areas of our lives. What do *you* do more than others? Are you above average? Do you excel? Are you uncommon in any realm of your life?

Let's take that basic appeal from the Word of God and apply it to three vital areas of our lives—our work lives, our moral lives, and our home lives.

Be Above Average in Your Work

First, *a Christian ought to rise above the average in his work life.* A Christian ought to be more diligent, faithful, honest, and conscientious in his work and in his relationships with other people at work than a person who is not a Christian. Being a Christian ought to cause us to rise above the average, whether we are an employer or an employee.

How does the average person approach his work today? I think he generally approaches it as drudgery to be endured rather than a pleasure and a privilege to be enjoyed. It is a necessary evil—something that he must do. Therefore, he never really puts his best into it and so he never rises above the average.

A lot of people approach their work like the young man who joined the English army and volunteered for service in India. When asked why, he said, "Well, I understand that in India they pay you a lot for doing a little. Then when you've been there for a while, they pay you more for doing less. And when you finally retire, they pay you a great deal for doing nothing."

Many people seem to be looking for a job that pays them a great deal for doing practically nothing. When they find work they do not put their highest and their best efforts into it. They are content to be average.

Being a Christian ought to cause a person to improve both the quality and the quantity of his work. It ought to make him more diligent, faithful, honest, considerate, understanding, helpful, and more generous than a person who does not know Jesus Christ.

The Apostle Paul made a marvelous appeal to both labor and management when he told slaves to be good hard workers, not just when the boss is watching but at all times. He told them to go about their work as though Jesus Christ were their foreman, and God were their paymaster—for in reality that is the case (Col. 3:22-25). If a person is a Christian, then Jesus is Lord of all his life. This includes what he does at work.

If you are an employer you are to be honest and just. You are to be fair. You are to be considerate of your employees at all times, remembering that God is your Master (Col. 4:1). That's the difference that being a Christian ought to make in a person's work.

In the Capitol building in Washington, D.C. is a statue of Crawford W. Long, the medical doctor who discovered sulphur ether and its values as an anesthetic for medicine and surgery. Inscribed on it are his words, "My profession is to me a ministry for God." Every Christian ought to feel that way. We should look on our professions as opportunities to serve both man and God. The way we do it, the spirit in which we do it, the quality and the quantity of our work should all be testimonies to the fact that Jesus Christ makes a difference in our lives.

So the appeal of Scripture is that both workers and employers rise above the average. Ask yourself Jesus' question: "What do ye more than others" on the job? At home? In the classroom? We need to rise above the average.

Be Above Average in Your Morals

Then, *we need to rise above the average in our moral lives.* People ask me occasionally, "Are the morals of America getting worse, or is the news coverage getting better?" I think that it is both. Our national morals are worse today than ever before. Statistics prove this is so. To make matters worse, the news media picks up on many of these things and instantaneously spreads them around the world. This widespread news publicity makes evil and immorality more commonplace. After a while some people justify their wrong actions by saying "Everybody's doing it." I've heard people try to justify everything from smoking marijuana to premarital and extramarital sex, divorce, and abortion by saying, "Everybody is doing it."

That's not true. Not everybody is doing immoral deeds. It is true that many people are doing them. It may even be true that most people are doing them. It is probably true that most of the people you associate with are doing them. But it is not true that everybody is doing these wrong deeds. But even if it were true, when and where did we ever get the idea that right and wrong are determined by the number of people who do a thing? The majority is not always right.

Let the average person choose between the Beatles and Beethoven and who do you think would win? Let the average person choose between Shakespeare and the Late, Late Movie and which would get the higher rating? The majority can be wrong. A case in point is Jeb Stuart McGruder. He was a promising politician with a good background and a great future. But he looked around him in Washington in the days of Watergate and saw that everybody was doing it. So he did it too. He covered up the truth. When he was sentenced to prison, someone asked him why he did it. He said, "My ambition obscured my judgment. Somewhere between my ambition and my ideals I lost my compass."

We all need a compass with which to sail the seas of this life. Ours must not be the majority opinion or the Gallup Poll. It must be the eternal Word of God. Pornographic pictures, dirty books, and magazines are becoming more and more prevalent. Subtly, television writers and producers are working in nudity, permissiveness, profanity, perversion, and provocative dialogue. The harmful effect of this is enormous. People, especially the young, see these chic, sophisticated people behave immorally and they think this must be the thing to do! Kids, you know, are indelibly impressed by what they see attractive, famous people do, even on TV.

How do the writers justify this kind of moral irresponsibility? They say, "We're only depicting life as it is." But look at it this way. Garbage is also a part of life as it is. It is a part of realism. We have garbage cans at our house. However, we feel that it is best to keep our garbage cans in the backyard with lids on top of them. We could, if we wanted to, put our garbage cans on our front porch. That's our right. And we could, if we wanted to, bring the garbage cans into our living room and take their lids off. But life goes better if the garbage is kept out of sight and out of smell. Much entertainment today is moral garbage that is being dumped into our minds and into our homes. The end result is that it is not depicting life as it is, but it is depicting too much of the rotten side of life.

In a world like this, "What do ye more than others?" Do you have a different moral compass? We Christians should rise above the average in our moral values and conduct.

Someone has said that everybody is born an original and dies a copy. Too many of us let society reduce us down to average. And this includes lots of God's people.

A word of warning though. If you decide to rise above the average, you are in for problems. You are headed for conflict, for society keeps trying to bring everybody down to average.

Look at Calvary. There were three crosses there. On two of them were common criminals. On the other one was the Son of God. Society was saying to the criminals, "You level up. You're below average and we don't like this." And they were saying to the Son of God, "You level down. You're above average and we don't like that either."

Later, look at the Philippian jail. Inside it were criminals. But the Apostle Paul and his fellow worker Silas were also there. Society is always saying to its criminals, "Level up." And to its saints, "Level down. We want everybody average."

If you attempt to live above average morally and spiritually, there will be those who will want to bring you down. But remember, if you are flattened by an opponent, you can get up again. But if you are flattened by conformity, you are more likely to stay down. Let's rise above the average morally.

Be Above Average in Your Marriage

Finally, *we need to rise above the average in our marriages*. Splitsville is the fastest growing community around. Every day finds the highway that goes there more crowded. The distance between the marriage altar and the divorce court is closer than it has ever been before. Our homes are in trouble. Psychiatrist Don Jackson, after an intensive investigation of many marriages, estimated that not more than 5 to 10 percent of all married couples enjoy a really good relationship. About 40 percent of all marriages end in divorce. And a large percentage of those who don't get a legal divorce are experiencing an emotional divorce. They still live in the same house, eat at the same table, and may even sleep in the same bed, but they are miles apart emotionally. They stay together for the sake of the children, or for economic reasons, or out of religious conviction, or because of social pressures. In a society where that is the average, "What do ye more than others?" What kind of relationship are you building? What kind of home life do you have?

Dr. David Mace says that three things are necessary to build a good marriage. The first is a commitment to growth. A commitment to permanence alone is not enough. We need to be committed to grow in our relationship together. At best all we do is bring raw materials into a marriage. We lay the foundation in courtship. And we usually lay a pretty good foundation because we try so hard to impress the other person. If we would keep on trying that hard all the days of our marriage, we would have a wonderful relationship. But most people lay a good foundation in courtship and then quit building, so the relationship deteriorates.

Second, you need to have a good communications system. You need to share your deepest feelings with one another. Communication is both giving and receiving a message. If there is no communication there is no relationship. The only way to keep any relationship alive is to communicate.

Third, you've got to make constructive use of conflict. All marriages have some conflict. The question is, how is that conflict going to affect you? Are you going to be destroyed by it? Or are you going to use it to build a better relationship?

There are three ways that you can deal with any conflict. There is the hot war approach. You can shout and scream and seek to destroy one another.

There is also the cold war approach. You can give each other the cold shoulder. You can ignore one another. You can become pouty, sullen, silent, and moody.

There are two ways to defrost a refrigerator. You can use a blow torch. That will do it. Or you can just unplug it. That will do it too. The end result is the same. You can kill a marriage just as quickly by becoming sullen, pouty, and moody as you can by shouting and screaming. The end result is that the marriage dies.

But there is a third and better way to deal with conflicts. Any two mature, intelligent, Christian people ought to be able to sit down and negotiate peace. You don't have to wage a hot war or a cold war. You can use your conflict to build the relationship. The problem with most people is that they aren't trying. If things don't work out, they walk out. In this kind of society, "What do ye more than others?"

Rising above the average—that's what we need. In our work, in our morals, and in our marriages, God wants us to excel.

What about you? You say, "I'm afraid that I'm just average, but I would like to be better. Do you have any help for me?"

Yes, I have help. It's in Jesus. He is the only resource of the Christian life. It's not enough to read a book. It's not enough just to want to be helped. It's not enough to attend church regularly. You've got to get in touch with and walk with Jesus Christ, through reading His Word and talking with Him in prayer. When you are walking daily with Christ, conscious of His presence, and leaning on Him for strength and guidance, He'll lift you above the average.

7

Called to Greatness

Alfred Adler, one of the fathers of modern psychiatry, said that one of the dominant impulses that every human being is born with is the instinct to get ahead. It seems to be a part of our natural equipment and there is no way to get rid of it.

We are not surprised then when we hear disciples James and John ask Jesus if they may be His chief assistants when He would rule the world (Mark 10:37). This request reveals their self-seeking ambition. They were not satisfied just to be a part of His kingdom. They wanted to be His two top men. They wanted the highest places of prominence and importance in God's kingdom.

I hope this doesn't disappoint you in James and John. The difference between the best of men and the worst of men is not their instinct but the goals and ends to which they are directed. The greatest saints have always been made of the same material as the greatest sinners. Though desire and the ambition to get ahead can ruin us, none of us would amount to anything without them. Most of the progress of mankind can be traced to people's ambitions and their desires for greatness.

It led astronauts to the moon, despite many obstacles. It keeps scientists in their laboratories and it keeps missionaries on their fields of service.

The answer is not to destroy ambition but to employ it for good. Ambition can be like a river that runs wild and destroys the land. Then you can put up some flood control dams and control it. That's what we need to do with ambition—channel it, direct it, but not destroy it altogether. Jesus did not condemn ambition; He redefined it and sought to redirect it.

Jesus recognized that everybody is born with the desire to excel, to get ahead, to be successful. Jesus therefore did not condemn it, or rebuke it, or forbid it. Rather He challenged us to employ it for good. He urged us to reach for true greatness. Sin lies not in a desire for greatness but rather in the shabby, pathetic ways in which we sometimes reach for it.

Our problem is that we tend to measure greatness in terms of power, wealth, and prominence. We Americans tend to think of life as a pyramid. To most of us the really great people are the ones who have managed to scramble to the top of the pyramid. The higher one climbs, the more people there are under him and thus the greater he is.

The people of Jesus' day were much the same. Power, authority, and wealth were what they respected and desired most. Rome, like a giant octopus, encircled most of the world. Her military and economic tentacles possessed crushing power. Field commanders wielded disciplined soldiers as an expert chess player handles pawns. Any person or group that demonstrated a threat to established governmental power was quickly eliminated.

Local politicians sold their integrity to Rome for a measure of power. Life was cheap. Jewish men spat the word *servant* as they did the word *leper* or *Gentile*. Often a person's social status was measured by the number of slaves he owned or the number of lives he controlled.

Even the religious leaders of Jesus' day had a warped view of greatness. So He warned His followers to beware of the scribes and Pharisees who enjoyed going around in long robes and who sought the best seats in the synagogues. They too were competitive, self-seeking pyramid-climbers.

In today's freewheeling age, when many people work themselves into ill health, wreck their homes, and step on and over people to climb to the top in our fiercely competitive culture with its emphasis on success, wealth, and prestige, we need to recognize and to rethink what Jesus had to say about true greatness.

Jesus said that in the kingdom of God greatness is measured in terms of service. The greatest people are those who serve the most. The solution to our problem then is not to stifle our desire for greatness. It is to redirect it, to channel it for good. Christ's call to commitment is a call to true greatness. It is a call to the kind of humble service that He himself came to render. Jesus' call teaches us that to achieve true greatness there is a price to be paid, a paradox to be accepted, and a person to be imitated.

The Price of Greatness

When James and John made their request for places of prominence in His kingdom, Jesus asked if they were able to drink the cup that He would drink and to experience the baptism that He would experience (Mark 10:38).

The cup (10:39) is a metaphor for the life and experiences that God hands out to people. Jesus prayed, in the Garden of Gethsemane, "Father, if it be possible, let this cup pass from Me" (Matt. 26:39).

The word *baptism* (Mark 10:39) means to submerge in any experience. Both of the last two references allude to the suffering experience that Jesus would endure before and during His crucifixion. Jesus was in essence saying to James and John, *"If you want to wear the crown, you must first bear the cross. You cannot succeed unless you bleed."* Jesus was telling them that He would earn His right to reign. They must also be willing to pay the price if they were to reign (10:39).

Success and greatness have their price tags. Lee Bickmore, president of the National Biscuit Company, once talked about the "price tags of success." He said, "No man can become a great leader, or a great success, on an eight-hour day." He added that the price for greatness in the business world is long hours and some sleepless nights. It is push, push, push.

However, in the kingdom of God the price tag of success is different. It starts with surrender to God's will. It includes service to others and self-denial. You must deny yourself and lose your life in God's service if you want true greatness.

Jesus once said, "Among them that are born of women there hath not risen a greater than John the Baptist" (Matt. 11:11). If you want a clear picture of Christ's estimate of greatness, you would do well to study the life of John the Baptist. He is greatness personified. He is greatness in flesh and blood.

Who was John the Baptist? He was a hard-hitting, straight-shooting preacher who stirred revival fires around Israel in preparation for the coming of Christ. Hundreds of years before John, Malachi had said that before the great and dreadful day of the Lord, Elijah would come and turn people back to God. John the Baptist was the Elijah foretold by Malachi. He wore the same garb and lived in the same kind of isolation. He had the same courage, the same grim, gaunt strength, the same fiery energy. And Elijah, Ahab, and Jezebel have their doubles in John, Herod, and Herodias.

John came out of the wilderness preaching, "Repent! Turn from your sins and turn back to God." Then he told people to be baptized to show their sincerity, their genuine sorrow over their sins, and their desire to be ready for the coming Messiah. John feared no man. If a thing needed to be said, he said it. He had a reputation for telling it like it was. The popularity of John the Baptist was immense. Whenever he preached, merchants closed their shops and the cities emptied to hear him. When the Pharisees saw his popularity, they courted him. Herod, the king, heard him preach happily and often. A lesser man might have succumbed to this popularity, flattery, and applause and compromised his message. He would have been tempted to play to the galleries and keep the momentum of his popularity, but not John. He was no pyramid-climber. The Pharisees were snakes in the grass and John told them so. Herod was living in adultery and John denounced him for it. John cared not for his own popularity, fame, or self-advancement. He cared only for what God wanted him to do.

When people asked him, "Are you the Christ?" he replied, "No! I am just a voice, that's all. There is One coming after me whose sandals I am not worthy to untie." That's humility!

When Jesus came to be baptized of John, John said, "Lord, I shouldn't baptize You. You should baptize me." But Jesus prevailed and John baptized Him. As Jesus entered into His public ministry, the crowds turned from John and began to follow Christ. He moved into the forefront and John began to fade from the scene.

One day a group of disciples came to John and said, "I guess you know that Jesus is drawing greater crowds than you. And His baptismal record is greater than yours also."

Lesser men might have become jealous and envious. But not John. He said, "That's the way it should be. He must increase and I must decrease." There was no self-seeking in John. He took the role of a servant. He lived only to honor and to obey God and to magnify the Lord Jesus Christ. It was humble service that marked John the Baptist.

Wherein lay John's greatness? It was in his explicit obedience to the will of God. It was in his genuine humility. It was in his willingness to die to himself, to take the role of a servant, and to magnify Jesus in everything.

When I die to myself I no longer am responsible for being successful. I'm just responsible for doing God's will and working day by day and hour by hour in His kingdom. It is His business whether I have a big ministry or a little one. He is the Chairman of the board. I am just pleasing Him.

The Paradox of Greatness

Greatness through service is a paradox, an apparently contradictory statement. Jesus often taught by using paradoxes. He said once, "The meek shall inherit the earth" (Matt. 5:5). That's not what we normally believe. We believe that the mighty, the wealthy, the strong, those who push, push, and push will inherit the earth. But Jesus said it belongs to the meek.

He also said, "It is more blessed to give than to receive" (Acts 20:35). We don't ordinarily think that. Most people are more interested in what you can give them than in what they can give you.

Jesus also said, "Whosoever will save his life shall lose it" (Matt. 16:25). We most often think that if we want to find our lives then we must grab for all we can get. We must pour every ounce of our strength into getting ahead. But Jesus said that if we would lose our lives in His great cause then we would receive them back again.

There is no greater paradox than the one Jesus gave James, John, and us in this experience. He said that in the unbelieving world greatness is measured by the amount of power, influence, and control a person has over other people (Mark 10:42). The greater a man is, the more people there are under him. But in the kingdom of God, this is not the correct measure of greatness. With God, greatness is not measured by authority, power, or rule. It is measured by service (10:43-45).

We need to change our values. They are so often distorted that we really do not know what is important. I once read of a backwoodsman who was being examined by a physician for an insurance policy. He was asked several questions about his brothers and sisters and other aspects of his family background. When the physician began to ask questions about his father, however, his face took on a long look. He said to the physician, "My father is dead." The physician then asked the cause of his father's death. Being afraid that he might lose the insurance, he replied, "I don't know just what it was that killed him, but it warn't nothing serious."

Many people today don't realize what is important and what is not. Calvary is a great example. Men thought that Calvary was a defeat, but God knew that it was a victory. What we think is a failure may be our greatest success.

We think of position or wealth as signs of greatness, but they are not. Money and privilege do not make anyone great. They only give us opportunities to be great. We must use whatever wealth and power and privilege we have in serving others if we are going to be really great.

The epitaphs of great men reveal this. A few years ago I stood at the small family cemetery where Thomas Jefferson is buried. On his tombstone was the epitaph he had written himself. It said, "Here was buried Thomas Jefferson, author of the Declaration of American Independence, of the Statutes of Virginia for Religious Freedom, and father of the University of Virginia."

It did not say that he had been the Governor of Virginia, Minister to France, Secretary of State, and President of the United States. Why? He told his daughter, "The things that are not on my inscription are things the people did for me. The things that are on it are those things that I did for the people."

The same was true of George Washington Carver. He was one of America's greatest scientists. He was born a slave. When he was freed by the Emancipation Proclamation, he went to college and earned a degree from Tuskegee University. Following graduation he went to work for the college for $125 a month and stayed there for the same salary the rest of his life. He often turned down as much as a $100,000 a year from such men as Henry Ford and Thomas Edison because he believed that it was God's will for him to develop the commercial possibilities of Southern agricultural products. When he died they put this simple epitaph on his grave: "He could have added fame to fortune, but caring for neither, he found happiness and honor in being helpful to the world."

The last sentence on the tomb of Chinese Gordon in St. Paul's Cathedral holds the key to his great life. It reads, "Who at all times and everywhere gave his strength to the weak, his substance to the poor, his sympathy to the suffering, and his heart to God."

The greatness of all these men was in serving.

The Personification of Greatness

Jesus' life demonstrated this principle. He said, *"For even the Son of man came not to be ministered unto, but to minister, and to give His life a ransom for many"* (Mark 10:45). He Himself is the supreme illustration of greatness.

Bruce Barton once asked a great historian, "You have viewed the whole panorama of human progress. What heads arise above the common level? Among them all, what half dozen men deserve to be called great?"

The historian turned the question over for a day or two and then gave Barton a list of six names with his reasons for each. It was an extraordinary list. The names he gave were Jesus, Buddha, Asoka, Aristotle, Roger Bacon, and Abraham Lincoln.

Think of the thousands of emperors who have battled for fame. Yet Asoka, who ruled in India centuries before Christ, is the only emperor on that list, not because of his victories but because he voluntarily abandoned war and devoted himself to the betterment of his subjects.

Think of all of the people who have struggled for wealth. But no millionaires are on the list with the exception again of Asoka. The historian, when he was seeking for something that has endured, found the message of a teacher, the dream of a scientist, the vision of a seer. "These six men stood on the corners of history," the historian said. "Events hinged on them. The currents of human thought were free and clear because they had lived and worked. They took little from the world and left much. They did not get; they gave."

That Jesus should be considered great or even numbered among the great by a non-Christian historian is a miracle.

Jesus never did the things that usually accompany greatness. He accumulated no fortunes, He led no armies, He ruled no countries, He wrote no books. Yet He is the greatest Man who ever lived. He is great not only because He is God's Son, but also because He served.

Who were considered the great men in Jesus' day? Caiaphas! Herod! Pilate! Yet we would never have heard of them but for their association with Christ.

This then is greatness. It is forgetting about yourself and serving other people. When Christ calls us to commitment, it is to this kind of humble service. It is a call to forget ourselves and lose ourselves in ministering to others. That is the greatness we are to strive for.

8

Called to Witness

During the days of World War I, the United States was having trouble with German submarines. We did not know how to deal with them. Will Rogers offered a solution. He said, "What we need to do is to boil the ocean. This will create such a pressure that it will force the submarines to the top. Then it will be as easy to destroy them as shooting ducks on a pond."

A reporter replied, "That's a good idea, Will, but how are we going to boil the ocean?"

Will Rogers answered, "I'm just telling you what to do. It's up to you to work out the details."

This approach is often used in talking about evangelism. We talk about it in such vague generalities that when we get through everybody knows what to do but nobody knows how to do it.

Jesus told us that He came to seek and to save those who are lost (Luke 19:10). Later, He said, "As My father hath sent Me, even so send I you" (John 20:21). Christ's call to commitment is a call to be a witness. It is a call to reach out after the lost and attempt to bring them to the Saviour. To fulfill our mission we must know how to do this well. Jesus, the Master evangelist, not only told us that we should evangelize the world, but He also showed us by His own ministry how to do it.

The Gospels tell us about a few of the active days in the life of Jesus. He kept busy traveling about the cities and the villages teaching, preaching, and healing. As He went about this work, the sight of the multitudes moved Him to compassion. The word *compassion* means to "suffer with, to feel the same thing as." As Jesus moved among the people, He was moved by the people. He felt what they felt. He suffered as they suffered. He entered into and shared their deep hurts and distresses.

These experiences led Jesus to point out to His disciples that the harvest was abundant but that the workers were few. Then He told them to pray that God would send more workers into the fields. Jesus had hardly finished telling His disciples to pray for more workers when He called His 12 apostles, instructed them, and sent them out to meet the very needs He had just pointed out (Matt. 9:35—10:15).

In this encounter the Lord shows us the essentials of evangelism. In it we see the practical things that we need to do to carry out our basic mission. Three things are necessary to win our world to Christ: Insight! Enlistment! Infiltration!

See the Need

The first essential to evangelism is insight. We must see the world as Jesus saw it. The Scriptures say, "When He saw the multitudes, He was moved with compassion on them, because they fainted, and were scattered abroad as sheep having no shepherd" (Matt. 9:36).

The evangelistic efforts of Jesus began when He saw the deep spiritual needs of the people. What He saw moved Him to action.

What did Jesus see when He looked at people? The words "fainted" and "scattered" tell us. These two words indicate that Jesus looked beyond the external and outward appearances of people and saw the deep agony of their souls. The word translated *faint* means "to grow feeble." It suggests the idea of falling out as a result of weakness. When Jesus saw the multitudes, He saw them beaten down, defeated, and whipped by life. Does this remind you of anybody you know?

The word translated *scatter* means to "break one's unity or completeness." A shepherd holds his flock together. Jesus saw the multitudes in His day as having no shepherd. They had lost the integrating center of their lives. They had lost that which holds life together, so their lives were fragmented and falling to pieces. Does this sound familiar? Every day a good counselor sees people like that.

What was the reaction of Jesus to all of this? He was moved with compassion. He literally felt what they felt. He entered into their experiences with them. What He saw moved Him to action. There is no greater motivating force in the world than compassion. To see human needs through eyes of love is to be moved to action.

Many others saw the same multitudes that Jesus saw, but they did not see the same thing. The Pharisees saw the crowds only as chaff to be burned in the furnace of God's judgment. The disciples saw them too but they saw them only as a nuisance to Jesus. But when Jesus looked at them, He saw beyond their outward appearance. He saw their spiritual needs and longings. He saw their lostness.

Many years ago a shoe salesman was sent to Africa to sell shoes. He had been there only a few weeks when he wired his home office: "Send me a ticket for home. Nobody over here wears shoes." The home office brought him back.

Then they sent another man. He had been there only a few weeks when he wired back: "Send me more shoes. Everybody over here needs shoes."

The two salesmen saw the same bare feet, but they viewed them differently. One saw obstacles and impossibilities; the other saw opportunities and needs.

There is a lot to be said for the way you look at things and people. Look around you. What do you see when you see the multitudes? Don't be fooled by those Hollywood suits,

Ralph Lauren dresses, and plastic smiles. In and behind many of them are people who are hurt, heartbroken, lonely, and lost. Like the multitudes of Jesus' day, a sizable percentage are beaten down and defeated by life and their lives are falling to pieces. Unless you see these deep spiritual needs, you will never do anything about meeting them. You will never be moved to compassion. You will never do a great work of evangelism, for evangelism begins with this kind of spiritual insight.

"What can I do," you ask, "to improve my spiritual sight or insight?" For one thing, you can walk in close fellowship with God. You can get so close to the Lord through prayer and Bible study that you begin to see the world through His eyes. Secondly, you can move among the multitudes as Jesus did. To see people who are lost or who have heartaches and illness will move you to want to do something about it. And you will do something, unless your heart has become cold and calloused. But if you just sit in the comfort of your home and church and do not move among people, you will not be moved by the people.

Enlist the People

The second essential to evangelism is enlistment. We must recruit people to meet the needs. Once we see the needs of unconverted people, we realize that the job is too big for any of us to do alone. We must have help. Jesus saw the multitudes and was moved to compassion for them. But He realized that the crowds were too vast and the needs were too great to be met by one person. So He urged His disciples to pray that God would send forth more people to help meet these needs (Matt. 9:38). The first inclination of our hearts ought always to be to pray. Prayer ought not to be a last resort. It ought to be our first response.

Jesus had hardly finished urging His disciples to pray when He called them and trained them and sent them out to meet these needs.

Look at the 12 men Jesus chose. There was not a seminary-trained man in the group. None of them was a religious professional. Four of them were fishermen. Who can do anything with a fisherman? One was a tax collector. Israel was occupied territory at this time. It had been conquered by Rome, and now Roman legions were garrisoned in every major city. They were there to enforce Roman law and to protect Roman property. Wherever Rome ruled, it taxed the people heavily. Taxation was usually carried out through local officials. Local citizens were hired by Rome to collect taxes on a percentage basis. These tax collectors were considered traitors by their own people. They had turned against their own nation and had gone to work for the enemy. Many of them were unscrupulous, greedy, dishonest men. Matthew was one of these despised and hated tax collectors.

Then there was Simon the Zealot. The word *zealot* describes his political affiliation. He was a member of a nationalist party which had sworn to throw off the Roman yoke. These political fanatics were one-man guerrilla bands that opposed Rome.

These were three of the kinds of men Jesus called to be His disciples. These were men Jesus trained to be evangelists. They were not extraordinary men. They were men from different walks of life. They were from different economic positions and different political persuasions.

It was as if Jesus were saying, "Give me 12 ordinary men who will obey Me and follow Me, and I will turn the world upside down." If Jesus did not try to meet the needs of the world by Himself, neither should we. If He needed to involve other people, so do we.

Elton Trueblood said that we have projected the idea today that the church is a group of people streaming to a shrine to make up an audience for a speaker. Nothing could be farther from what the church is supposed to be. It should never be just an audience. The church should be a laboring crew charged with the responsibility of gathering in harvests of lost souls.

Somebody else has said that we have raised up an army in which nobody fights but the generals. If he's right, what a tragedy! We must awaken to the fact that the fields are ripe unto harvest. We must realize that they are so vast and the needs are so great that no one person and no few people can meet those needs alone. The "average" Christian must be enlisted in the task of gathering in the harvest of lost souls for God. The pastor must be looked on as a foreman who helps train, equip, and prepare people for the work of evangelism. Unless we enlist many more Christians in meeting the needs of the lost world, those needs will never be met.

Infiltrate the World

The third essential to evangelism is infiltration. We must get out of our church and go where the people are. The Scriptures say, "These 12 Jesus sent forth" (Matt. 10:5). Sent forth where? Out into the cities and villages where the people were.

When Jesus spoke these words, there were so many priests working at the temple in Jerusalem that they had to take turns serving. When the angel appeared to announce the birth of John the Baptist, Zacharias was working the 3 to 11 P.M. shift at the temple. But while these priests were keeping the fires poked up, the brass polished, and the sacrifices burning on the altar at the temple, the world was perishing without God. The multitudes were no longer coming to the temple to worship. It had become a den of thieves instead of a place of prayer. Does this sound familiar? Not many lost are coming to our churches today either. So we too must go after them. If we just sit in our comfortable sanctuaries and wait for people to come to us, we will never do the work of evangelism. The lost simply are not going to come.

Many churches today remind me of a laboring crew trying to gather in a harvest while they sit in the toolshed. They go to the toolshed every Sunday and they study bigger and better methods of agriculture, sharpen their hoes, grease their tractors, and then get up and go home. Then they come back that night, study bigger and better methods of agriculture, sharpen their hoes, grease their tractors, and go home again. They come back Wednesday night and again study bigger and better methods of agriculture, sharpen their hoes, grease their tractors, and get up and go home. They do this week in and week out, year in and year out, and nobody ever goes out into the fields to gather in the harvest.

You can't gather in the harvest while sitting in the toolshed. Somebody has to go out into the fields and work if the harvest is to be saved.

Some churches also remind me of the man who owned an oil well that pumped continuously. But his neighbor noticed that he never sold any oil. One day he got up enough nerve to ask the man why. He said, "I see your well pumping day in and day out, week in and week out, month in and month out, year in and year out. But I never see you selling any oil. How do you explain this?"

The man replied, "It's simple. It takes all the oil that we produce just to keep the machine going."

Many of our churches are like that. They dissipate all of their energy and their effort on internal affairs. They spend so much time keeping all of the committees functioning and the bylaws up-to-date and the air conditioning running, and the services in proper order that they have no time or energy to get out in the fields to do the work of evangelism.

The greatest purpose of most organizations is to survive. It ought to be to produce. If they cannot produce, then they ought to be allowed to die natural deaths. We ought not to keep them alive by artificial means. To let some organizations die would be mercy killing in the best sense of the word.

I'm not suggesting that we ought to abandon all organizations. That would solve nothing. Activism is better than most any other heresy. And in every technique there is some waste. What we need is a new dedication and a new list of priorities. We need many people with insight enlisted in the kingdom of God, and infiltrating the world for Jesus Christ. This is the only way we will ever do the work of evangelism.

There can be no evangelism without infiltration. We must get out of the church and into the world where the people are. Then we must share with them face to face the Good News of Jesus Christ.

After I have said all of this, the real question is, "What are you going to do about it?" If you do nothing, then this will be just another session in the toolshed. It will be just another time when we have studied bigger and better methods of agriculture and then have done nothing about it.

Edward Everett Hale once said, "I am only one. But I am one. I cannot do everything. But I can do something. And because I cannot do everything, I will not refuse to do the something that I can do." We must make that same resolve. Do what you can where you are today to win someone to Jesus Christ. This is a big part of what it means to answer Christ's call to commitment.

9

Called to Prayer

Archbishop Trent said, "Prayer is not overcoming God's reluctance; it is laying hold of God's highest willingness." He meant that prayer is not a battering ram by which we storm the gates of heaven and get God to do things He doesn't want to do. It is opening our hearts and lives to God, to allow Him free access to do what He very much wants to do.

Christ's call to commitment includes a call to prayer. God calls us to seek Him, His will, and His way in every area of our lives.

God has linked Himself to prayer, so when His people call on Him He hears and He helps. Jesus taught us this in the Parable of the Persistent Widow. The story Jesus told was of a widow who was in great distress. A businessman was trying to take advantage of her and take that which was rightfully hers. Women in general and especially widows in the first century were at the mercy of unscrupulous men. So this lady took the only recourse she had. She went to a judge and appealed to him to protect her, to defend her, to see that she got what belonged to her.

But the judge she went to was an unscrupulous man. He was a man without principle. He had no fear of God, and he had no regard for his fellowman. He thought only of himself. He really was not interested in other people and their needs. He was an unbelieving, cold-hearted, calloused man.

He couldn't have cared less about this poor widow who came to him for help. So he turned her away. But she came back again and again and again. Finally the judge said to himself, "Because this widow keeps bothering me, I will see that she gets justice, so that she won't eventually wear me out." And he did (Luke 18:1-8, NIV).

Jesus taught us a lesson from this story. He said that if this unrighteous judge could finally be moved to help this poor lady in need because she continually bothered him with her request, how much more our heavenly Father will render justice and help to His children who continually call on Him.

This is a teaching by contrast. Jesus did not intend that the heavenly Father be compared to this judge, because the judge was an uncaring man. He was calloused and indifferent. He answered the lady's request only to get her to stop bugging him. Jesus is not saying that God is like that judge. No, not at all. God is just the opposite. But if this indifferent and calloused man could eventually be moved to help a needy lady, how much more can the heavenly Father be moved to help us when we are in need, if we will come to Him and make our requests known.

This parable is a great encouragement to prayer. We all have long periods of seemingly unanswered prayer. We all go through periods of darkness when the heavens seem like brass. But Jesus urges us to stay with prayer. Don't quit. God can be moved and prayer is the force that moves Him. As Jesus encourages us to pray He teaches us three great truths about prayer:

A Sacred Duty

First, Jesus teaches us that *prayer is a sacred duty*. He said that we "ought" to pray. The word *ought* implies a moral obligation, a sacred duty. We have been told all of our lives that prayer is a privilege. It is. It is a wonderful, glorious privilege. To be able to take our needs, our burdens, and requests to the Lord of heaven and earth is an incomparable privilege. But prayer is more than a privilege. It is also a responsibility. It is a sacred duty placed on every one of us by the Lord Jesus Himself.

God tells us many things that we *ought* to do. For one thing, He tells us that we ought to give our money regularly and generously to support His work (1 Cor. 16:2; 2 Cor. 9:6-7). Giving is a sacred duty.

Then the Bible teaches that we *ought* to obey God rather than men (Acts 5:29). If we are ever forced to choose between obedience to God and obedience to men, we must be true to God. That is a solemn responsibility.

And Paul taught us that those who are spiritually, financially, and physically strong *ought* to bear the infirmities of the weak (Rom. 15:1). We are to be sensitive to the needs of others. It is a spiritual obligation.

We are also told in the Scriptures that husbands *ought* to love their wives as Christ loved the church (Eph. 5:25-28). As Jesus died for His church without murmuring and complaining, so ought men to gladly and joyfully sacrifice for their wives. To obey this command would radically change most marriages and homes.

Finally, John says that we *ought* to love one another (1 John 4:11).

These are just a few of the *oughts* of the Christian life. But remember this, the obligation to prayer is just as much a duty, a responsibility, as any of these *oughts*. Prayer is an *ought* that is on a par with every other Christian duty. Just as surely as we ought to give, and we ought to love, and we ought to live right, and we ought to help people, so we ought to pray.

Why did Jesus say we ought to pray? It is because He knows what prayer can do. Prayer can change a life. Prayer can save a soul. Prayer can revive a church. Prayer can empower a person. Prayer can turn a life around. Jesus, knowing what prayer can do, said people ought to pray.

The Apostle Paul endured many hardships as a mission-ary. His life was often threatened and he faced constant danger as He preached the Gospel of Christ. But he wrote to thank his Christian friends by saying, "You have helped us through your prayers" (2 Cor. 1:11). That's interesting. Prayer is a way to help people. In fact, it might be the most effective way to help people. It may be far more effective than giving a person $20. It may be much better for you to pray for your child than for you to do many other things you could do for him. Is it any wonder then that Paul urged us to pray for everyone? (1 Tim. 2:1)

It isn't any wonder that when Saul, the king, came to Samuel, the prophet, to beg him not to quit praying for Israel that Samuel answered, "God forbid that I should sin against the Lord in ceasing to pray for you" (1 Sam. 12:23). These all believed that prayer was not only a privilege but also a divine obligation. We cannot escape the fact that we "ought always to pray" (Luke 18:1).

A Constant Need

Jesus not only tells us that prayer is a sacred duty, but He also teaches us that *prayer is a constant need*. He said that we "ought always to pray." The word *always* means not only at all times but in every circumstance of life. Nothing in your life that is worthwhile, that is important, ought to be outside the circle of prayer. We ought to pray about every circum-stance and every need in our lives.

Most of us feel that there are certain times and certain situations in our lives that merit prayer more than others. If someone in our family is gravely ill, we know we should pray. If we are going to have surgery, then we know we ought to pray. If we are facing some great decision, or if we are having difficulty in our marriage, or if our children are in trouble, these are times when we need to pray. We know that there are certain times and certain situations when we ought to pray.

But Jesus is saying to us here that if we only understood

life correctly we would know that we ought "always" to pray. Even at those times when we do not feel the need to pray, we still need to pray. Prayer must never be left to our feelings alone. We must pray even when we don't feel like it.

Let me illustrate. When do I need to pray more? When I am about to be wheeled into the operating room for surgery, or when I'm about to leave town and go on a vacation? Most of us would say that we need prayer the most just before surgery. But no, we need prayer equally at all times. The fact that I'm about to have surgery only intensifies my awareness of my need. I need God on my vacation just as much as I need God in the operating room. The difference is not in my need; the difference is in my awareness of my need. We usually think we can make it by ourselves on our vacations. But we are not so sure about making it by ourselves through serious operations.

When do I need God more? When I'm going to have a quiet dinner with my wife, or when I'm preparing to speak to a large audience? Most of us would think that we'd need God more when we are preparing to speak to a large crowd. But the fact is that I need God as much at one time as the other. True, I need God to preach an effective sermon, but I also need God if I want to spend a quality evening with my wife. I need God not only in my public proclamations, but I also need God in my private family relations.

I dare not leave prayer to my feelings. I pray when I don't feel like it as well as when I do feel the need. And believe me, there are times when I don't feel like praying. Prayer is not to be left to the inclination of my heart. It is to be a discipline in my life. I should pray at all times and for all of my needs because I recognize my total dependence on God.

One of the great men of prayer was George Mueller. He operated orphanages in England years ago and he did it by faith. He never told anybody about his needs for money. He just prayed and God laid the needs on people's hearts. As a result, money for his orphanages came from out of nowhere—or better still, it came from above.

One day a friend watched as Mueller was trying to write a letter. He was having great difficulty and so he bowed his head and prayed. When he lifted his head and his friend asked what he was doing, he said, "Well perhaps you noticed that I was having trouble writing this letter. The pen point was scratching the paper and I wanted the letter to be right. I was just asking God to help me write the letter as I should."

His friend replied, "I can't believe it! A man who trusts God for millions is also praying about a pen point."

We can all understand why people pray in their times of crises. We can also see why people would pray for large amounts of needed money. But the pen points of life are important to God also.

Jesus is inviting us to bring *all* of our needs to Him—to live continually in dependence on and in close relationship with Him. Prayer ought not to be our last resort; it ought to be our first resort. We ought not to wait until we are in a desperate situation and then cry out to God. We ought to pray all the time. People ought always to pray.

A Practical Necessity

Finally, Jesus tells us that *prayer is a practical necessity.* He said that people ought always to pray and "not to faint" (Luke 18:1). The word translated *faint* means to "lose heart, to grow weary, to fall out."

Actually there are two possible meanings to the phrase "and not to faint." The first and most obvious is that we are not to give up or quit in our praying. We are not to be prayer dropouts.

However, another meaning is possible. It could also mean that we are to pray so that we will *not* "fall out" in the difficult task of living.

Jesus recognized that life is hard. Pressures, hardships, and disappointments come to all of us. If we aren't careful they can destroy us.

All around us are people who have been overcome by the

pressures of life. Jesus presents an alternative to that in this parable. Through prayer we can find strength and power that will enable us to stand up to life.

It is good to believe in yourself. Everyone needs self-confidence. But you don't live long until you discover that by yourself you are not adequate for life. You need other people and you need God. You need strength and resources outside yourself. Prayer is the link that connects us with the heavenly Father, who can do all things.

Often the only two alternatives in life are to pray or to faint. When we pray, we receive the strength we need for the battles of life.

Former President Eisenhower was raised in a Christian home. His parents read the Bible to him. They taught him to pray and prayer sustained him in life. In his biography he tells of those times in World War II when, before great battles in the darkness of the night, he would go out to some windswept hill and talk to God. The awful burden of commanding an army, of having the lives of young men in his hands, weighed heavily on him. In his talks with God he found strength for the battles.

In the dark days of the Civil War, a visitor in the White House heard a low rumbling coming from the President's room. As he walked down the hall in the darkness of the night, he saw President Lincoln on his knees by his bed. He was praying a prayer something like this, "Oh God, Thou who didst hear Solomon as he cried out in the night for wisdom, hear me, for I cannot lead these people and I cannot govern this nation without Thee. I am weak and sinful and helpless. Oh God, hear me and help me—and save this nation."

And it may very well be that the salvation of our nation was sustained and sealed by the President on his knees. Strength for the battles of life and for our homes and for our nation comes from God through prayer.

Jesus anticipated the response of His audience that day. Some of them were bound to say, "How do we know God will hear and will help?" So He closed this teaching by saying, "Nevertheless, when the Son of man cometh, shall He find faith on the earth?" (Luke 18:8)

What did Jesus mean by that? He was saying, in effect, "It is not a question of whether or not God has the power to answer your prayer. The question is, Do you have enough faith to offer up a prayer?"

The burden of proof is not on God; it is on us. God has been answering prayer since the beginning of time. The issue of prayer is no longer up for debate. The real question is not God's faithfulness, but our faith. It is *not* "Does God have the power to answer?" but "Do we have the faith to ask?" It is not His willingness but our willingness.

The greatest evidence of faith is prayer. The first prayer that a person ever prays effectively is for God to forgive his sin, because Jesus died to pay for it. That's the cry of faith, the cry of commitment, the cry of surrender. And after having called on God in faith we are to live a life of faith, continually drawing on His strength. That's one thing He calls us to do when He calls us to commitment.

10

Called to Action

There is a great deal of fuzzy thinking today about what it means to be good. This is because most people think that being good means not being bad.

Let me illustrate. A mother is going to the grocery store and she plans to leave Jimmy at home with his little sister. She says to him, "Jimmy, you be good while I'm gone."

But that's really not what the mother means. She really means, "Jimmy, don't be bad." She doesn't want Jimmy to get in a fight with his sister, or to break a window with a baseball, or to twist the cat's tail. She doesn't want Jimmy to be bad, but she says, "Jimmy, you be good."

There are many people like Jimmy's mother. They believe that being good is the same thing as not being bad. They think that if you don't do a lot of bad things, then you are good.

When Jimmy's mother comes home from the store she asks, "Jimmy, have you been good?"

Jimmy replies, "Yes, Mother, I've been good." With that Jimmy indicates that not only does his mother not know the difference between being good and not being bad but neither does he. When Jimmy says, "Yes, Mother, I've been good," he doesn't really mean that. He doesn't mean he has been helping out an elderly person, or that he mowed the grass, or that he carried out the garbage. Probably all he did was curl up on the couch and watch television. But the fact that he hadn't done anything bad led him to say, "I've been good."

No person is good solely on the basis of what he does *not* do. There is a big difference between being good and not being bad. Christ's call to commitment is a call to a life of goodness. We must make the most of our possibilities, opportunities, and trusts. It is not enough not to be bad. Jesus calls us to be good in an active sense. He calls us to action.

This truth is an underlying principle that is found in many of Jesus' teachings. For instance, Jesus told a story about a wealthy man who planned to take a long trip into a foreign country. So he called in his employees and committed his possessions to them. To one man he left five talents, to another he left two talents, and to another he left one talent. A talent was a huge sum of money. It was equal to a laborer's yearly wage. He told these men to use his wealth to make a profit while he was gone.

Then the wealthy man left the country. The servant who had received five talents immediately invested his money. He made a good investment and doubled his master's money. The man who had received two talents did the same thing.

But the man who had received only one talent was afraid he might lose everything if he made an investment. He reasoned, "If I invest this money, I may lose all of it. This would incur the wrath of my master, so I will just hide his money in a safe place and keep it until he returns." So the third servant buried the money in a secret place to keep it safe until his master's return.

When the master returned he immediately called his servants in and asked for an account of their business dealings while he was gone. The servant who had received five talents told his master what he had done.

The master commended this servant and gave him a promotion by saying, "Well done, thou good and faithful servant. Thou hast been faithful over a few things; I will make thee ruler over many things. Enter thou into the joy of thy lord" (Matt. 25:21). He did the same with the second servant.

The master then called in the servant who had received one talent and asked for an account of his business dealings. The servant told the master that he was afraid of losing everything, so he buried the talent to keep it safe.

What do you suppose was the response of the master? He said to him, "Thou wicked and slothful servant, thou knewest that I reap where I sowed not, and gather where I have not strawed. Thou oughtest therefore to have put my money to the exchangers, and then at my coming I should have received mine own with usury" (25:26-27).

Then he told his other servants to take the talent from this man and give it to the servant who had 10. "And," he said, "cast ye the unprofitable servant into outer darkness. There shall be weeping and gnashing of teeth" (25:30). Notice the three words that Jesus used to describe this man. He called him wicked, slothful, and unprofitable.

These are strong words. So strong, in fact, that we might feel that the master was too severe with this man. After all, what was his great sin? He did not embezzle his master's money. He did not spend one cent of it on riotous living. He would never do anything like that. He was not that kind of man. And when he was asked for an account of what he had done, he told his master the complete truth. What then was this man's sin? His sin was not so much in what he did, but in what he failed to do. He wasn't bad. He was just good for nothing.

Jesus told this parable to spotlight that third servant. Jesus' point is that we should not spend our lives in idleness, laziness, and indifference if we expect the commendation of our Lord when He returns. This parable challenges us to get busy and work until Jesus comes again. If we do nothing good, even though we are not bad, the Lord considers us as wicked, slothful, and unprofitable.

Let's look carefully at Jesus' indictment of those who do nothing:

They Are Wicked

First, *the person who does nothing is wicked.* The word *wicked* is a very strong word. Jesus seldom used it. He didn't refer to the woman taken in adultery as wicked. He didn't call Zaccheus, the crooked tax collector, wicked. He didn't call the thief on the cross wicked. But He did call the third servant wicked. Jesus used it only two other times. He used it once to describe a man who owed a creditor about $10,000. When the time came for the note to be paid the man couldn't pay. When the creditor found out that the man was not going to pay the debt, he threatened to take the man's wife and children as slaves, which was a common practice in those days. The debtor fell down on his knees before his creditor and begged for mercy. His creditor was so moved with compassion at the pleading of this man that he canceled the debt and forgave the man all that he owed.

Then the man who had been forgiven immediately went to see another man who owed him a meager sum of money. He took the man by the collar, shook him soundly, and said, "If you do not pay me the money you owe me, I will have you thrown in jail." When the poor man could not pay the debt, the forgiven man had him jailed.

When Jesus described this man who had been forgiven of a $10,000 debt but would not forgive someone who owed him only $100, Jesus called him "wicked" (Matt. 18:32).

On another occasion Jesus used the word *wicked* to describe the Pharisees, the religious leaders of that day. Pharisees were exact in their observance of all of the laws and traditions of their religion. But many of them were proud, insincere, and inconsistent. Many or most were cold and calloused to the needs of people around them. And they were continually trying to embarrass and discredit Jesus. When they did this the Scriptures tell us that "Jesus perceived their wickedness" (Matt. 22:18).

Why did Jesus call the wealthy man's third servant wicked? Because, by his own admission he knew what was expected of him and he did not do it. And if a person knows the good he ought to do and does not do it, he sins (James 4:17). Jesus considers this do-nothing wickedness comparable to the wickedness of being unforgiving and being judgmental.

To fail to obey a good command is as bad as doing a forbidden evil. Both are disobedience against God. The same God who said "Thou shalt not" also told us many things we should do. To ignore God's positive commands is as much a sin as to violate His negative ones. Not all the wicked people in town are in the bars or jails or porno places. Many of them come to church Sunday after Sunday, sit in comfortable pews, listen to beautiful music and biblical sermons, but never do anything about them. This too is wickedness.

They Are Wasteful

Jesus also called this man "slothful." The word *slothful* means lazy. Solomon said that *a man who "is slothful in his work is a brother to him that is a great waster"* (Prov. 18:9). So a lazy person is a wasteful person.

This servant excused himself by saying, "I was *afraid* and did nothing."

But his boss said, "You were *lazy* and did nothing." How many times do we excuse our laziness by calling it something else? We say that we are afraid, or we are timid, or we are busy, or we do not have ability, or we do not know what to do. We make all kinds of excuses for doing nothing when the real reason is that we are lazy.

In what sense is a person who does nothing wasteful? He is not making the most of his opportunities, talents, and potentials. For all practical purposes these things are wasted. Nothing ever comes of them so he might as well not have them.

Thomas Edison was probably the greatest inventor in history. He invented the phonograph, the incandescent light bulb, the microphone, the mimeograph machine, the medical fluoroscope, the nickel alkali battery, and hundreds of other things. However, Thomas Edison had every reason to do nothing. At the age of seven his mother took him out of a private school because his teacher had said Tom was "addled." He had only three months of formal schooling. Gradually he lost his hearing until he was almost deaf. And he failed in many more experiments than he ever succeeded at. So he could have wallowed in self-pity. But not Edison. He got busy and taught himself the things he needed to know. When people asked if his deafness was a handicap, he replied, "No, how many things have you heard today that weren't worth listening to?" In fact, he capitalized on his deafness because it shut out noise and enabled him to concentrate more.

When a friend once asked if he weren't discouraged over a project that had failed about 10,000 times, he replied, "Why, I have not failed. I've just found 10,000 ways that won't work."

Think what a waste it would have been if Thomas Edison had done nothing. He would not have had to do bad things. It would have been sufficient for him to do nothing. The world would have been worse, and we would all have been losers if Edison had taken life easy.

I think God must often feel like Abraham Lincoln, who once wrote to General McClellan, "If you are not planning to do anything with the army, will you lend it to me for a while?" I think Christ may feel like saying to us today, "If you aren't planning to do anything with your talents, your potentials, your opportunities, give them back to Me so I can use them."

Unfortunately many professing Christians are of no use to the Lord. Note that the first two men in this parable used 16 words to tell what they had done. The third man used 43 words to try to explain why he hadn't done a thing.

Doing nothing is a serious sin because it is a sin against both knowledge and opportunity. When confronted by his master, the servant said, "I knew that you are a hard man . . . " You might have expected him to say, "I knew that you are a hard man, so I worked real hard." But not so. He said, "I knew that you are a hard man . . . and I was afraid."

The master replied, "You wicked, lazy servant! . . . At least you could have loaned the money out and let it draw interest. You had a great opportunity and you wasted it."

Ignorance is not our main problem. Everywhere I go I find people who know what they ought to do, but they do not do it. Our problem is not our minds but our wills. We lack dedication. We don't need to *know* better; we just need to *do* better. We need more devotion, not more truth.

They Are Worthless

Finally, Jesus called this man unprofitable. The word *unprofitable* means unserviceable, useless, worthless. *This man did nothing; therefore, he was worth nothing.* This does not imply that our worth to God depends totally on what we do. We each have a value, a worth to Him that is completely apart from what we do. We are all made in His likeness and that fact alone gives us value to Him. Even while we were sinners He loved us and Christ died for us (Rom. 5:8). The word *worthless* refers to kingdom progress. So far as that is concerned we are useless to Him.

Many in the kingdom of God are unprofitable. They are liabilities instead of assets. If the average car had as many useless parts as the average church, it would barely have enough power to run downhill.

Every one of us ought to be good for something. D. L. Moody was a great evangelist. He was to his generation what Billy Graham is to ours. Moody was untrained and uneducated. He had been converted by a Sunday School teacher while working as a clerk in a shoe store. God blessed his life and ministry so much that he rose to international prominence.

Moody was preaching in a noonday service once. After the service was over a school teacher came up and said, "Mr. Moody, if I could not use the English language any better than you, I would not speak in public." Poor Moody did misuse the English language. His unedited sermons were absolutely atrocious. But Moody looked the teacher in the face and kindly said, "Lady, I know I make a good many mistakes." And then he humbly and quietly added, "But I'm doing the best I can for Jesus with what I have. What are you doing for Jesus with what you have?"

On another occasion someone criticized Moody for some of the methods he used in doing things. His reply was classic. He said, "I don't like them too much myself. What methods do you use?"

When the critic said that he used none, Moody tartly retorted, "Well, I think I like the way I do it better than the way you don't do it."

Of course the people who are doing nothing are usually the most critical people in the world. That's because they have time on their hands. They are not involved in a meaningful activity and therefore they can sit around and find fault with those who are working.

The penalty for being unprofitable is loss of opportunity. If you wish to lose all that books have to offer, it is not necessary that you burn all the libraries in the world. All you need to do is to leave the books alone.

If you want to destroy your marriage relationship, it is not necessary for you and your mate to fly at each other's throats. All you have to do is to neglect each other. Never compliment one another. Never help one another. Never be courteous. Just do nothing.

If you wish to destroy or lose the finest friendship in the world, you need not insult your friend. All you need to do is to leave him alone.

If you want to destroy your flower garden, you need not plant weeds in it or rip out all the beautiful flowers. All you need to do is to leave it alone.

The same is true of your relationship with the Lord. You don't have to get angry at Him or curse or insult Him. All you need to do is to go your own way, ignoring God and His Word. You will then forfeit your opportunity to serve the Lord for you will be unprofitable to Him.

We dare not miss the message of this parable. We are to stay busy until we die or Jesus returns, whichever comes first. If we fail to use our opportunities and talents we will miss our Lord's commendation.

Eleven months before his death, Billy Rose gave his 105-piece collection of modern sculpture to the state of Israel. As Prime Minister David Ben-Gurion received it he asked, "If we are ever attacked, where do you want us to hide your bronze statues?"

Rose didn't hesitate a minute. "Don't hide them," he said. "Melt them down into bullets."

In these critical days, the saints of God do not need to be displayed like bronze statues, or stay hidden in places of safety. We need to be melted down into bullets, to penetrate our sinful world for the kingdom of God.

11

Called to Fullness

Many psychiatrists say that the vast neurotic misery of the world could be termed "a neurosis of emptiness." The evidences of boredom, futility, and emptiness are everywhere. The spiraling suicide rate, increased consumption of alcohol, growth of the drug traffic, and people's endless pursuit of pleasure are all expressions of a deep boredom with life—and an inner emptiness. These are all just symptoms of our basic problem. For the people who do these things are but the children and grandchildren of the "hollow men" that T.S. Eliot wrote about a half century ago. These things only reflect an inner hunger and thirst for a satisfying, fulfilling life. It is emptiness that fills the bars, the highways, the lakes, amusement parks, the divorce courts, and the jails of our day.

Emptiness is always dangerous. A man must be filled with something! For human nature, like physical nature, abhors a vacuum. If a man is not filled with God, then alien forces will flood in to fill the vacuum in his soul. An empty life is susceptible to all kinds of evil.

Jesus once told a weird and spooky story which makes just that point. He said, "When the unclean spirit has gone out of a man, he passes through waterless places seeking rest, but he finds none. Then he says, 'I will return to my house from which I came.' And when he comes he finds it empty, swept, and put in order. Then he goes and brings with him seven other spirits more evil than himself, and they enter and dwell there; and the last state of that man becomes worse than the first" (Matt. 12:43-45).

In this story Jesus compared a human personality to a house with an undesirable tenant. The owner evicted the tenant, fixed up the house, and left it clean but unoccupied. One day the old tenant came walking by. He went and peered in the window and saw that no one else was living there. So he found seven even wilder friends, and they broke in, took over, and completely wrecked the house and left it worse than it had been before.

There is much about demons that I do not understand. But the meaning of this story cannot be misunderstood. It points out the peril of emptiness. It teaches us that it is not enough to rid our lives of evil. We must also fill our lives with good.

A negative religion is never enough. But the faith of many people has not advanced beyond the negative. There are some Christians who are better known for what they are against than what they are for. They pride themselves in what they do *not* do. They may empty their lives of evil, but they fail to fill them with good.

We must never underestimate the importance of the negatives in the Bible. When Moses came down from the mountain he brought with him 10 great Laws. All but two of them begin with "Thou shalt not." We can't ignore these negatives.

Jesus and the apostles also preached negatives. When Jesus talked about unbelievers and their evil natures He said, "Do *not* be like them" (Matt. 6:8). The Lord Jesus told us *not* to lay up for ourselves treasures on earth, *not* to use vain repetitions in our prayers, *not* to parade our religion, and *not* to worry about the things of this world.

A life without negatives is like an automobile without

brakes. A car without brakes is headed for a wreck. A life with no restraints will end up a moral, spiritual, emotional, and perhaps a physical wreck.

But while negatives are important they are not sufficient. An automobile must have brakes to avoid disaster, but it must also have a motor and an accelerator if it is to be useful. We need not only to be able to stop. We also need to be able to go.

The Pharisees to whom Jesus often spoke were good examples of a negative religion and the peril of emptiness. They had emptied their lives of idolatry, but they had not filled their lives with the living God. So what happened to them? Hypocrisy, pride, indifference, and a judgmental spirit entered their lives to fill the vacuum. The end result was that many of them were worse in spirit than other people were in practice. They were worse off in the end than they were in the beginning. What they should have done was to have filled their lives with faith, love, humility, and good works. Then everything would have been well.

We face the same danger. We often become aware of our sins and vow amendment. We reform. The houses of our lives are swept clean but left empty. An empty house invites undesirable tenants. We should not only banish the demons; we should also welcome Jesus. A life filled with love for God and our fellowman leaves little room for evil.

Adam C. Welch loved to preach on the text, "And be not drunk with wine, wherein is excess; but be filled with the Spirit" (Eph. 5:18). When he did so, his opening sentence was, "You've got to fill a man with something." It is not enough to drive out evil. Good must come in. There are many people whose lives are empty. They are bored, frustrated, and are enduring a meaningless existence. Their lives need to be filled.

Christ's call to commitment is a call to fullness. It is a call not only to empty our lives of evil, but also to fill them.

What can we fill our lives with? There are at least three things:

Fill Your Life with God

There is a God-shaped vacuum in every one of us. Nothing else will fill it. *Without God there will always be an emptiness in our lives.* The tragedy of many lives is that people cut themselves off from God. Then life turns empty, and then sour. W.T. Montague said, "Atheism leads not to badness, but only to an incurable sadness and loneliness."

Years ago W.E. Sangster visited the United States. Someone asked him what impressed him most about our country. He said, "You seem to have more of everything than anybody else. You have more cars, more televisions, more refrigerators, more of everything. In fact, I've noticed that you also have more books on how to be happy than anybody else."

We are learning that nothing else but God can satisfy the deepest longings of the human heart. Not education, not pleasure, not material possessions, not even religion. It is even possible to have a church full of empty people.

Humans are the only creatures in the universe that are capable of being bored. All other creatures are content to exist. But men's and women's lives must be filled with meaning. People are the only creatures that experience emotional breakdowns. They are the only creatures that both laugh and cry because they are the only ones who know the difference between the way things are and the way things ought to be. Boredom and emptiness are both evidences of our higher heredity. They tell us that we were made for God. Until we find Him our lives remain empty. And empty lives are susceptible to depression, despair, immorality, and worse evils.

Don't leave your life vacant. A life without God falls prey easily to other evils. So let your life be occupied and ruled by God. Put your faith in Him and your life will be full.

What is faith? Faith is not belief without evidence. It is commitment without reservation. It involves the intellect, the emotions, the will, the whole person. Faith is not a leap into the dark. It is a step into the light.

There is abundant evidence for God. While His existence can neither be absolutely proven nor disproven, the evidence for God is overwhelming.

First, there is the evidence of nature. We do have the universe all around us. It demands an explanation. Where did it come from? Either it made itself or someone made it.

Could it have made itself? We know nothing else that made itself. The more we learn about the vastness and preciseness of the universe, the more convinced we are that it could never have "just happened."

The stars and the planets are innumerable. They move in space with more accuracy than the parts of a fine watch. The earth makes one complete revolution around the sun every 365 days, 5 hours, 48 minutes, and 46 seconds. The movement of the planets and stars is the most accurate measurement of time we have.

An accident? No! Professor Edwin Conklin said, "The probability of life originating by accident is comparable to the probability of the unabridged dictionary originating from an explosion in a printing factory."

Then there is the evidence of conscience. Even if we could explain the material universe without God, we would still have spiritual reality to explain. How do you explain conscience? A sense of right and wrong exists in all people, everywhere. Conscience could never spring from a mechanical universe or originate by chance.

Immanuel Kant said, "Two things fill my heart with awe and never-ceasing wonder: the starry heavens above me, and the moral imperative within me."

Finally, there is the resurrection of Jesus Christ from the grave. The Resurrection not only proves that He is the Son of God, but it is an evidence for God Himself. If there is a Son, there must be a Father. Jesus came to make the God of Creation and the God of conscience known to us through personal experience.

Study deeply enough and you will see that there must be a God. His existence is self-evident. That's why the Bible says, "The fool hath said in his heart, 'There is no God'" (Ps. 14:1). Through faith we can commit our lives to God as He is known in Jesus Christ. God then comes to fill our hearts and the emptiness is gone. As we live with Him we enjoy the peace, purpose, and power that makes life worthwhile.

Fill Your Life with Love

Nothing brings more lasting satisfaction to life than the joy of helping other people. Dr. Karl Menninger said, "Love cures people—both the ones who give it and the ones who receive it." The unhappiest people in the world are the ones who are living only for themselves.

No one finds life worth living; you have to make life worth living. If you will fill your life with love and service to God and to others, you will be putting into it those things that make life wonderful.

For over a hundred years managers have been tremendously interested in throwing out unnecessary labor and cutting down the hours necessary for production. Labor-saving devices, additional machinery, and more efficient methods of production were created to drive out the evil spirit of hard work. We succeeded in reducing the number of hours a person must labor in a day and the number of days that he must labor in a week. Now leisure has come to all classes of people, except workaholics. The average person has twice as much away-from-the-job time as he has laboring time.

But the larger question we are just beginning to ask is, "What are we going to put into this leisure time?" We have thrown out many of the old drudgeries, but what are we going to put in their place? If we fill those hours with drinking, pleasure-seeking, and television watching, we will find ourselves worse off than before. As Dave Garroway said, "If something doesn't happen, the next generation will have eyes the size of saucers and brains the size of a split pea." Idleness never develops the best that is within us.

Quite to the contrary we soon become bored and unhappy.

Some time should be given to rest, some to relaxation, some to self-improvement, some to worship, and some to volunteer service. A life that is empty of labor can lead to a worse condition than before. We've got to fill our lives with love and service. George Small once said, "I read in a book that a man called Christ went about doing good. It is very disconcerting to me that I am so easily satisfied with just going about."

Let's stop dead still for a moment and ask ourselves, "Is there a single person who can look me squarely in the eye and say, 'I thank God for you — my life is better because of you — I'm glad you are living'?"

Would anybody say that of you? If you were to die to-night, would it be much of a loss to anybody?

Fill Your Life with Hope

A third ingredient that we need in our lives is hope. What is hope? It is joyful expectancy. What oxygen does for our lungs, hope does for the meaning of our lives. Dr. R. McNair Wilson, a cardiologist, wrote in his autobiography, "Hope is the medicine I use more than any other."

Everywhere in the Bible we are taught that there is a life to come. The Bible does not argue for its existence or try to elaborately explain it. It just declares it. Gordon Allport says, "The future is what concerns people most of all." Without hope for the future the present would be unbearable. There is hope in Christianity. Nothing can take that away.

But Christ gives us more than just hope for the life to come. He also gives us hope in the present. Since World War II an Austrian psychiatrist, Victor Frankl, has written extensively on the relation of the meaning of life to the whole structure of personality. He claims that the need to find meaning in life is more basic to a human being than pleasure or power or anything else. The thesis he repeats again and again is that if a person has a "why" to live he can endure almost any "how." But if that dimension of "why" is lacking, then the whole structure of one's life eventually collapses.

This insight into the importance of meaning was developed by Frankl during the years he spent as a Jewish prisoner in a German concentration camp. Life there, of course, was unbelievably harsh and brutal. The prisoners were forced to work long hours and were given barely enough food, clothing, and shelter to survive. As the months unfolded Frankl began to note that some prisoners soon collapsed under the pressure and gave up and died, while others under the same conditions continued to cope and managed to stay alive.

Using the tools of his psychiatric training, he would talk in the evening to scores of his fellow inmates about this and he found a pattern beginning to emerge. Those prisoners who had something to live for, that is, an objective that gave a sense of meaning to their lives, were the ones who tended to mobilize their strength and survived.

Their objectives varied widely. One prisoner had a retarded child back home, and he had a great desire to get back and take care of that one. Another had a girlfriend he expected to marry as soon as the war was over. Frankl himself had begun a book and had a fierce desire to survive and finish it and get it published.

These were all reasons that made sense to the individuals themselves, meanings that welled up from within them, rather than being superimposed from without. And the existence of such "whys" to live enabled them to cope with the awesome "hows" of that prison situation. On the other hand, Frankl found that those prisoners who had no sense of meaning "soon gave up" and either succumbed to disease or voluntarily took their own lives. Out of this actual experience, Frankl came to believe that having a meaning in life more than anything else is what makes us and keeps us human.

The lesson of Jesus' story about the empty house is simple. It's not enough to cleanse our lives. We also need to invite the Holy Spirit in, to fill our lives.

As Dale Evans says, "All of my life I looked for a pot of gold at the end of the rainbow, but I found it at the foot of the cross." You can find it there too.

12

Called to Faithfulness

The first professional football game I ever saw was a real thriller. It was between the Houston Oilers and the Baltimore Colts, in Houston's Astrodome. In no time at all the Oilers found themselves behind 21-0. Then slowly but surely, the Oilers fought back until they tied the game.

With 1 minute and 15 seconds left on the time clock, Baltimore punted to the Oilers. Then methodically the Oilers moved down the field and kicked a field goal to go ahead. With only 30 seconds left on the clock, Houston then kicked off to Baltimore. Baltimore ran two or three quick plays and ended up on their own 45-yard line with three seconds left to play. It looked like the Oilers had the game won, and everyone seemed to relax, including the Oilers' defense. On the last play of the game the Baltimore quarterback faded back, his wide receiver raced down the sideline, and the ball and the receiver arrived at the same place at the same time—and Baltimore won the game on the last play of the game. The crowd sat there in disbelief. They were stunned to see the game lost on the very last play.

Former President Eisenhower said, "When you are in any contest, you should work as if there were—to the very last minute—a chance to lose it. This is battle, this is politics, this is anything."

This sums up the truth of Scripture: "He that endures to the end shall be saved."

The New Testament records Jesus' saying this twice. He said it the first time to His disciples as He was preparing to send them out to preach and teach in His name. Perhaps bright visions floated in their minds of the honor and esteem they would receive from people. Lest they should start their work without having counted its cost, Jesus gave them a full description of the kind of treatment they might receive. They could expect rejection, hatred, persecution, and even death. Then He reminded them that it is not the commencement of their ministry, but the completion of it that is so important. Jesus said, "He that endureth to the end shall be saved" (Matt. 10:22).

The second time Jesus made this statement was in the context of His teachings about the end of the world. He told us that we can expect wars, famines, earthquakes, and pestilence as the end approaches. And we can also expect persecution, rejection, and even efforts to kill us. False prophets will abound and their followers will be many. And there will spread over the world a chilling indifference. Then He added, "But he that shall endure to the end, the same shall be saved" (Matt. 24:13).

Jesus made it clear that the battle of a Christian's life is stern. We are striving against spiritual powers. Our life is one of continued warfare. We may contend even unto blood. We must stay faithful till the final gun. We must not quit until the last play is over. If we follow Him we are always striving, never ceasing, always plowing the stormy seas, and never resting until the end of our life or the end of time.

The Christian life is not a sprint but a marathon race. It is not an isolated skirmish but a long campaign. Jesus said that those who remain loyal and steadfast and faithful to Him will be saved.

Today there are many who joined the Christian army long ago but have ceased to fight. They have deserted or defected. They entered the Christian race, but they dropped out before the finish line. We all need to hear this warning again.

The kind of commitment Jesus calls us to is the kind that lasts. It endures. It doesn't quit, and neither should we. We should not drop out, but remain faithful until the end.

The Demands of Faithfulness

This verse (Matt. 10:22) makes it clear that *Jesus demands endurance*. Who shall be saved? Not all who are confirmed, not all who can recite the Apostles' Creed, not all who have been baptized, not all who are members of the church, but those whose faith endures to the end.

This does not mean that it is our own endurance that saves us. There is but one plan of salvation. We are saved by God's grace through faith (Eph. 2:8-9). Grace is Jesus' dying on the cross for our sins. It is God's reaching down His hand of love, acceptance, forgiveness, and salvation. Grace is the father of the prodigal son waiting anxiously and lovingly for his boy to return and then welcoming him home with open arms. Faith is believing in, adhering to, and relying on Jesus Christ as Lord and Saviour. It is committing oneself to Him. God's grace is always conditioned on our receiving His Son by faith.

This verse (Matt. 10:22) describes the kind of faith that saves. It is the kind that endures, that hangs on, that remains loyal. Saving faith has an enduring quality. Common sense tells us that just having an emotional experience with God is not enough. In such a country as ours, most people have had at least one religious spasm in their lives. Real faith not only begins but it remains faithful to the very end.

Jesus is here striking at shallow emotionalism. He did that often. Once Jesus told a story about a farmer who went to sow his field in grain. In those days planting was done by the broadcast method. The farmer would take a handful of seeds from a sack and scatter them out in front of him as he walked along. Naturally, he would not have precise control over where the seeds fell.

Jesus told us about a man who went forth to sow a field (Matt. 13:3-23). Some of the seeds fell by the wayside, some fell on stony ground, some fell among the thorns, and some fell on good soil. The wayside was a hard and beaten path through the field. It had been made that way by people who walked it day after day and kept it packed down. The seeds that fell on this hard, packed ground were unable to penetrate it. In time the birds came and ate those seeds.

Some of the seeds fell on stony ground. This was land with a thin layer of topsoil over a layer of bedrock. The seeds would sprout and grow, but because there was no depth to the soil, they could not sink their roots very deep. So when the hot sun beat down on them, they withered and died.

Other seeds fell among the thorns. These would be in the hedgerows along the edge of the field. The seeds sprouted and grew momentarily, but soon the weeds and thorns choked the life out of them.

Only a few of the seeds fell on good ground and were productive.

Jesus told this story not to teach us a lesson in agriculture but to teach us a lesson in human nature. He explained that just as there are different kinds of soil that receive seeds in different ways, so people make different responses to the Gospel.

Many people are like the stony ground. They make shallow and emotional responses to Jesus Christ. That's because they fail to think things through. They are at the mercy of every new message, fad, or craze. They are quick to take up a new thing and just as quick to put it down. Some people's lives are littered with things they begin and never finish. Jesus is saying that our response to the Gospel and our commitment to Him must be so deep and so abiding that it causes us to endure to the end.

This is *not* to suggest that a person must be perfect in order to be saved. Years ago a famous artist painted a rugged picture of a pioneer wagon train. It was nighttime and the covered wagons had been drawn into a circle for safety. A campfire lit up the center of the circle and the men were gathered around it. The leader of the wagon train had a map spread on the ground in the light of the campfire and he was kneeling by it. He had on a red flannel shirt. His beard was uncut, his rolled-up sleeves exposed his huge arms, and his shirt was open at the neck. On the map was a heavy black line that zigzagged halfway across the page. It marked the way they had come. The heavy black line showed that they had veered north and then south, but their main direction was west. Evidently there had been an argument about which way to go from there. But the leader, with determination in his wearied features, placed his finger on the end of the black line, and his other arm pointed out toward the dark, hazy mountains. He seemed to be saying, "We may have to go south around a mountain, or north across a river, but our main direction will be west."

It is direction of life and not perfection of life that matters most. If we are saved from our sins, our lives will be Godward in direction. There may be times when we drift off course momentarily, but we will soon come back. If our faith is not strong enough to keep us moving in a Godward direction, it is not strong enough to save us.

Difficulties of Faithfulness

There are always difficulties to be endured if we are to remain faithful to Christ. The contexts of the two endure-to-the-end statements by Jesus are those of hardships, persecutions, and difficulties. Those who followed Jesus to the end in the first century had to be willing to endure all of these things. That made it hard to be faithful. It is still that way in many places in our world today.

Another thing that makes Christian living difficult is the inconsistent lives of God's people. Those who continue to walk in a Godwardly direction must climb over the fallen carcasses of inconsistent Christians. That's why it is important we keep our eyes on Jesus and not on those around us.

The Apostle Paul says, "Whosoever believeth on Him shall not be ashamed" (Rom. 10:11). The word translated *ashamed* literally means "put to shame, embarrassed, or disappointed." If we look to other people, we will often be embarrassed, ashamed, and disappointed. But in Christ there are no disappointments.

The greatest difficulty in remaining faithful to Christ comes from the temptations of the world. Paul spoke some sad words about one of his followers when he said, "Demas hath forsaken me, having loved this present world" (2 Tim. 4:10). We can almost hear Paul weep as he writes these words. Demas is mentioned three times in the New Testament. First, he was Paul's faithful helper during his imprisonment in Rome (Col. 4:14). Then he was listed in the group Paul called "my fellow laborers" (Phile. 24). Later Demas abandoned Paul and the work of God because he loved the present world more. Demas, the fellow laborer, became Demas the deserter. Bit by bit, the fellow laborer fell in love with the world—its goals, its allure, its pleasures. Then came that awful day when he deserted the cause of Christ.

John tells us that the world is made up of physical appetites, the desire to accumulate things, and arrogance. Lust, greed, and pride are the roots of all sin (1 John 2:16).

Perhaps some modern-day Demas is reading these words. You may be a young person who was once loyal to Christ while you were at home. Under the eye and the wing of your parents you attended Sunday School and church and were faithful to Christ. Then you moved away to college or some other place and in your newfound freedom you turned away from God and went after things of this world. If the last page of your spiritual diary were written today, it would read, "You have forsaken Christ, having loved this present world more."

Or you may be a businessman who was once active in God's service. You went to church faithfully. Your life and testimony counted for Christ. Then you bought a boat and it began to occupy more and more of your time. Or you got into a business deal that demanded more and more of your energy. Perhaps you started associating with the wrong people and doing their wrong things. If today someone carved your spiritual epitaph, it would have to say, "You have forsaken Christ, having loved this present world more."

Or perhaps you are a wife who once taught a Sunday School class and were involved in Bible study. Then you got caught up in a job, or in an endless round of social activities, until the spiritual things of your life were crowded out. If today your spiritual life were reduced to one sentence it would be this, "You have forsaken Christ, having loved this present world more."

The Lord demands that we believers be faithful to Him. But there are also difficulties to be endured. We dare not forget that "He that endures to the end shall be saved."

The Duration of Faithfulness

How long does God expect us to remain faithful? Jesus said we are to *endure to the end.* The Greek word for end is *hypomene.* It means "to the end of time" or "unto martyrdom." In the first instance Jesus is talking about the end of time. He is suggesting that we must be faithful until then. In the other passage He says that we may be hated, persecuted, and even put to death for His sake. There He says we must be faithful even to the point of death.

Whittaker Chambers, in his book *The Witness,* told about his involvement in the Alger Hiss case. In the section entitled "Letters To My Children" he writes, "In time . . . you will ask yourselves the question: 'What was my father?' I will give you an answer: 'I am a witness.' I do not mean a witness for the government or against Alger Hiss and the others. Nor do I mean the sort of squat solitary figure trudging through the impersonal halls of public buildings to testify before congressional committees, grand juries, loyalty boards, or courts of law. A man is not primarily a witness against something. That is only incidental to the fact that he is a witness for something. A witness in the sense that I'm using the word is a man whose life and faith are so completely one that when the challenge comes to step out and testify for his faith he does so, disregarding all risk, accepting all the consequences."

Chambers then pointed out that once someone asked him what it meant to be a Communist. He replied that when he was a Communist he had three heroes. One was a Russian. One was a Pole. And one was a German Jew. The Pole as a young man had been a political prisoner in Warsaw. There he insisted on being given the task of cleaning the latrines of the other prisoners. He did so because he held that the most developed member of any community must take on himself the lowliest task as an example to those who are less developed. This is one thing that it meant to be a Communist.

The German Jew was captured after a revolt and court-martialed. The court-martial resulted in a sentence of death. And the Communist said, "We Communists are always under sentence of death." That's another thing it means to be a Communist.

The Russian was not a Communist. He was a revolutionist against the Tsar. He was arrested for a minor part in the assassination of the Tsarist Prime Minister and sent into Siberian exile to one of the worst prison camps, where political prisoners were flogged. He sought some way to protest this outrage to the world. The means were few, but at last he found a way. In protest against the floggings of innocent men, he drenched himself in kerosene and set himself on fire and burned himself to death. That is also what it means to be a Communist. And then Chambers added, "That is also what it means to be a witness."

We Christians are all to be witnesses for Christ. The word *witness* is rooted in the idea of martyrdom. We are to endure and witness unto death for Christ. Some of you were once faithful to Christ, but you have deserted. You have defected and dropped out. But there is hope for you. You can come back. Our God is the God of a second chance. You not only *can* come back, but you *must* come back and *will* come back if you are to be happy in your life.

Robert Robinson, author of that magnificent hymn "Come, Thou Fount," became worldly and backslidden in his later life. One day he was riding on a crowded train. A young woman was seated by his side. She tried to engage him in religious conversation, but he was noncommittal. Presently she quoted the words of his old hymn, "Come, Thou fount of every blessing, tune my heart to sing Thy grace." It was too much for him. He broke down and wept and said to her, "Madam, I'm the unhappy man who wrote those words and I would give a thousand worlds to have the same joy that I had then."

Peter's life teaches us that a person can come back. He denied Christ, but after his confession he was recommissioned by Christ to be an apostle.

The life of John Mark also teaches us that a deserter can be restored. He was a young man when the church began, but he was at the very center of it all. It was at the house of his mother, Mary, that the early church met. When Paul and Barnabas set out on their first missionary journey, they took Mark with them as their helper (Acts 13:5). It looked as though Mark had embarked on a great career, but something happened. For some unknown reason, he went back home (13:13).

Paul took the defection very hard. Later when Paul was planning his second journey, he absolutely refused to take Mark along (15:36-40). Paul looked on Mark as a spineless deserter, and he refused to have him on his staff.

But years later Paul wrote to Timothy, "Take Mark, and bring him with thee, for he is profitable to me for the ministry" (2 Tim. 4:11). Mark had come back into fellowship and useful service. You can too. You can, and you will—if you really are a Christian. That's part of being committed to Christ. It means to be faithful. "He that shall endure to the end, the same shall be saved."

13

Called to a Cross

One of the most admirable things about Jesus is His absolute honesty. It is the kind of honesty that has characterized all great people.

After the siege of Rome in 1849, General Garibaldi, the great Italian patriot, made his famous proclamation: "Soldiers, all our efforts against superior forces have been unavailing. I have nothing to offer you but hunger and thirst, hardship and death; but I call on all who love their country to join with me."

In the days of World War II when Sir Winston Churchill became Prime Minister of England, he told his people that all he could offer them was "blood, sweat, and tears."

Jesus always calls people with that kind of honesty. No one could ever say that Jesus called him under false pretenses. Jesus never tried to bribe or lure people by offering them an easy way. He always made it clear that it was costly to be His disciple. He always set the demands high and then challenged people to follow Him by giving their highest and their best.

One example of this occurred when Jesus said, "Whosoever will come after Me, let him deny himself, and take up his cross, and follow Me" (Mark 8:34). And then Jesus added that it was only by losing our lives for His sake and for the Gospel's sake that we could ever find lives that are really satisfying and worthwhile (8:35).

After this He warns us that if we are ashamed of Him and His words in this adulterous and sinful generation, He will also be ashamed of us when He comes again in His glory (8:36-38).

This is a clear call to commitment. This call is summed up in Jesus' words, "Whosoever will come after Me, let him . . . take up his cross."

Remember that Jesus used two different symbols of commitment in His preaching. One was a yoke and the other was a cross.

The yoke is an implement of toil. The cross is an instrument of death. The yoke symbolizes service. The cross symbolizes sacrifice. In a yoke animals sweat as they pull the plow. On a cross men bleed as they die.

Christian commitment means that we are ready for either, the cross or the yoke. We are ready to pull at the plow or to die on the cross. We are ready to serve or we are ready to sacrifice. We are ready to sweat in toil or to bleed in martyrdom—whichever He may require of us.

The cross represented one thing—death and the suffering and pain that accompanied it. The cross was not merely a burden a person had to bear or some trouble that constantly plagued him. In Rome's day a convicted criminal carried his own cross to the place of execution. Then the cross was used as a means of capital punishment. It stood for death in the most agonizing way.

Jesus' use of the word *cross* in this passage suggests that if we are going to be His disciples we must follow Him with such absolute loyalty that we are ready to die for Him if necessary.

Jesus' use of the word cross helps us understand what it really means to be committed to Christ. It means that we must deny ourselves, dedicate ourselves, and declare ourselves.

Deny Yourself

Christian commitment begins with a funeral—when we die to ourselves and begin to live for Jesus Christ. Jesus calls us to this kind of dedication when He says, "If any man would be My disciple, let him deny himself." What does He mean by self-denial? A look at the background of this statement will help us understand it better. Jesus had just told His disciples that He must suffer and die in Jerusalem (8:31). Such a thing was unthinkable to His followers. So Simon Peter called Jesus aside and began to rebuke Him for talking that way. It was at this point that Jesus spoke these words about self-denial. He made it clear that He must not only go to the cross, but that if they were to be His disciples they must be willing to take up their crosses also.

For much of His life Jesus was engaged in a struggle between His own will and the will of God. That conflict was settled in the Garden of Gethsemane. There Jesus prayed, "Not My will but Thine be done." On His knees in the garden Jesus said no to Himself and said yes to God. Self-denial means exactly that—to say no to ourselves. It means to say no to our own desires, appetites, ambitions, and pleasures.

Self-denial is a practical expression of the lordship of Jesus Christ. It is so surrendering our will to the Lord Jesus that we obey Him and follow Him in everything.

To say no to self is never easy. It is contrary to our very nature. The essence of sin is selfishness. As Isaiah said, "All we like sheep have gone astray; we have turned every one to his own way" (Isa. 53:6). We all want our own way. We want to do our own things. We keep trying to assert our own wills. It is easier to say no to your children, to your wife, to your husband, to your boss, and even to the Lord than it is to say no to yourself.

An actor, in a newspaper interview, claimed that his bedroom has a mirrored ceiling because when he wakes up in the morning he likes to see someone he loves, trusts, and who cares a great deal about him. While his statement may have been tongue in cheek, more people feel like that about themselves than would ever admit it.

Indonesia's former President Sukarno once said, "I love my country, I love women, but most of all I love myself." You might insert something else in place of Sukarno's first two loves, but if you are honest you will probably have to say along with him, "Most of all I love myself."

There are two philosophies we may follow. We can choose to deny ourselves or we can choose to deify ourselves. We can become our own gods. We can govern our own lives. Or we may abdicate the thrones of our lives and let Jesus Christ be Lord. The choice is ours. But if we are going to be disciples of Jesus, we must begin by denying ourselves.

Dedicate Yourself

It is not enough just to deny ourselves. We can do that for any cause. All around the world there are revolutionaries who deny themselves for the causes of their revolutions. They risk their lives and live in deprivation for the causes they believe in. People deny themselves for such things as communism, athletic achievement, professional excellence, hobbies, fame, power, and politics.

So self-denial alone is not enough. *We must also dedicate ourselves.* Jesus said that we must lose our lives for His sake and the Gospel's. It is this dedication that keeps us loyal and obedient to Christ. When Jesus was crucified, His executioners drove huge nails through His hands and through His feet. But it was not the nails that kept Him fastened to the cross. It was His commitment. It was His surrender to the will of God. And it will be dedication that keeps us obedient to the cross also. For dedication is an act of personal choice. We are free to abandon the cross any time we choose. But if we are committed to Jesus Christ, we won't.

Bill Borden of the wealthy Chicago Bordens had as his motto, "Say no to self and yes to Jesus Christ every time."

Back in the days of the Great Society, President Lyndon Johnson was spending money faster than the government could print it. While he was funding all of his "Great So-ciety" programs, we were still in the middle of the Vietnam War. His aides began to pressure him to establish some order of priority for the government's vast spending pro-gram. He was advised that if the war continued, thus re-maining the number one task for the United States, then the "Great Society" should take second place. One of his aides commented, "Everything can't be put first as it has been."

Underline in your mind that statement, "Everything can't be put first." Now take it out of the realm of government spending and apply it to the way you spend your life. Some-thing or someone must take priority in your life. Everything can't be first. What is it with you? Is it your profession? Your family? Your recreation? Or is it God? Dedication demands that we put God first in our lives.

The real test of our dedication is what we are willing to lay on the line for the Lord Jesus. Luke describes Paul and Barnabas as men who hazarded their lives for the name of the Lord Jesus (Acts 15:26). The word *hazarded* is a gam-bling term. It means to place a bet, to make a wager, to lay something on the line. So Luke is describing these early missionaries as men who were betting their lives on God. They had laid their lives on the line for the Lord Jesus.

This is the real test of commitment. How far will you go for the Lord? What are you willing to risk for Him? The measure of your discipleship is not your theology, or your creed, or your giving record, or even your church atten-dance record. Your worth as a disciple is measured by what you are willing to risk for Jesus Christ. A true disciple is one who bets his whole life on Jesus Christ.

So Christ's call to commitment is a call to dedicate our-selves fully and completely to Him.

Declare Yourself

We must not only deny ourselves and dedicate ourselves but we must also declare ourselves. Jesus said that if we are ashamed of Him and His words in this adulterous and sinful generation, then He will be ashamed of us when He comes again in His glory (Mark 8:38). The word *ashamed* refers to our attitude toward Jesus.

One thing that leaps out from this passage is the confidence of Jesus. Though He had just spoken of His approaching death, He did not think for a moment that His death would be the end. He knew that He would be resurrected, that He would ascend into heaven, and that He would return again to earth. He was absolutely sure that in the end He would be triumphant.

So He set out a simple truth. When the King comes into His kingdom, He will be loyal to those who have been loyal to Him. If a person doesn't join in His battle today, he should not expect to share in His victory tomorrow. If someone refuses to serve in the Lord's campaign, he cannot expect to share in decorations after the campaign is brought to a successful conclusion. Following Jesus is often an unpopular thing to do. If a person is ashamed under such conditions to show that he is a Christian, if he is afraid to show which side he is on, he cannot expect to gain a place of honor when the kingdom comes.

This is a clear call to declare ourselves openly and publicly for Jesus Christ. Crucifixion was an act of public execution. Men were not crucified in the dark of night. They were not taken to a secluded place to be nailed to their crosses. Criminals were nailed on their crosses openly and publicly, not only to punish them, but also to teach passersby the consequences of violating Rome's laws. Crucifixion was a public act, intended to have a public impact.

All of this suggests that we cannot be secret disciples of Jesus. The Lord will not allow it. Jesus once healed a man who had been born blind. This act of healing was a clear demonstration that He is the Son of God. However, Jesus made one "mistake." He healed the man on the Sabbath Day. This was in violation of the Jewish tradition and so the Jewish leaders condemned Him.

They went to the man's parents and interrogated them.

They wanted to know if their son had actually been born blind and, if so, how had he been cured.

The parents were frightened. So all they would admit was that he was their son and that he had indeed been born blind. Beyond that they said they did not know anything. They told the leaders that if they wanted to know more they should go and ask him personally. He was old enough to speak for himself.

Then John comments, "These words spake his parents, because they feared the Jews; for the Jews had agreed already, that if any man did confess that He was Christ, he should be put out of the synagogue" (John 9:22). The fear of losing their social position kept them from confessing Christ.

Later John tells us that many among the rulers of the Jews believed on Jesus, but for fear of being cast out of the synagogue they did not confess Him. Then John comments, "For they loved the praise of men more than the praise of God" (John 12:42-43). Today there are still those who are more concerned about the opinions of people than about the opinion of God. Fear keeps them from openly declaring Christ as Lord.

After the crucifixion of Jesus, Joseph of Arimathea, who had been a secret disciple of Jesus, went to Pilate and asked for the body of Jesus so he could give Him a decent burial. Joseph believed on Jesus but out of fear of the Jews he had not confessed Him. However, when he saw Jesus die for him he could no longer remain silent. Joseph openly and publicly identified with Jesus (John 19:38).

Next (19:39) we are told that Nicodemus brought a large amount of expensive ointments to anoint the body of Jesus for burial. Was Nicodemus saved? Did he believe in the Lord Jesus Christ as his own personal Saviour? All we can say from the evidence is that we hope so. He had heard the great message of the new birth, but no record is given of any definite response that can be taken as positive proof that he had received Jesus' gift of eternal life.

It is true that Nicodemus once intervened to defend Jesus.

To the chief priests and Pharisees who condemned Jesus, Nicodemus said, "Doth our law judge any man, before it hear him, and we know what he doeth?" (John 7:51)

But this doesn't prove anything. There are many unsaved liberals who would say this much and more in defense of civil liberties. This is no proof of salvation.

After Christ had been crucified and His body was being prepared for burial, Nicodemus came with a magnificent gift of myrrh and aloes in accordance with the Jewish manner of burial and presented it for embalming the dead body of our Lord. All we can do is hope that this gesture came from a redeemed heart. We cannot know with certainty. Many stained-glass church windows have been installed because of guilty consciences. Nicodemus may be in heaven today, but we have no absolute proof of it.

How different it was with the woman at the well. After we meet Nicodemus (John 3), we meet her (John 4). There the Saviour gently and deftly reveals her lost condition to her. She sees herself as a sinner, she sees Him as the Messiah-Saviour, and she leaves her water pots to go back up the hill to the gates of the city in order that she may tell people, "Come, see a man which told me all things that ever I did; is not this the Christ?" (John 4:29)

And it is recorded that the Holy Spirit spoke through her renewed heart, and many of the Samaritans in that city believed on Him because of what this woman said (4:29-39). We have no doubt about this child of God. She was not stillborn; she made public her confession of Christ.

It is never easy to stand for Christ. Jesus said that people in A.D. 32 lived in an adulterous and sinful generation. Today morality seems to be even lower. The word *adulterous* means unfaithful. Many or most are unfaithful to God, to truth, to honesty, and to right. The word *sinful* means twisted, bent, perverted. Our whole age seems to be perverted and bent out of shape. But even in this kind of world we are not to be ashamed of Jesus.

During the Revolutionary War a young man came to

George Washington and said, "General Washington, I want you to know that I believe in you and your cause. I fully support you."

General Washington graciously thanked him and asked, "What regiment are you in? Under whose command do you serve? What uniform do you wear?"

"Oh," said the young man, "I'm not in the army. I'm just a civilian."

The general replied, "Young man, if you believe in me and my cause, then you join the army. You put on a uniform. You get yourself a rifle and you fight."

Jesus issues the same challenge to us today. He's not interested in sympathizers but soldiers. For this is the kind of commitment that leads to a worthwhile and satisfying life.